KIERAN EGAN

The Future of Education

Reimagining Our Schools from the Ground Up

YALE UNIVERSITY PRESS · NEW HAVEN AND LONDON

Set in Postscript Janson by Keystone Typesetting, Inc.
Printed in the United States of America.

Library of Congress Cataloging-in-Publication Data
Egan, Kieran.
The future of education : reimagining our schools from the
ground up / Kieran Egan.
p. cm.
Includes bibliographical references and index.
ISBN 978-0-300-11046-3 (cloth : alk. paper)
1. Education — Philosophy. 2. Teaching. 3. Learning.
I. Title.
LB14.7.E533 2008
370.1 — dc22   2008013246

A catalogue record for this book is available from the
British Library.

The paper in this book meets the guidelines for perma-
nence and durability of the Committee on Production
Guidelines for Book Longevity of the Council on Library
Resources.

10 9 8 7 6 5 4 3 2 1

CONTENTS

ACKNOWLEDGMENTS

I am grateful for the comments on the manuscript of this book made by a number of people, whose patience and kindness deserve a better reward than this. Members of the Imaginative Education Research Group at Simon Fraser University have read various chapters during our "writers' seminar" series. Gadi Alexander, Sean Blenkinsop, Anne Chodakowski, Daniela Elza, Mark Fettes, Natalia Gajdamaschko, and Stefan Popenici have been generous in the time they gave to reading parts of the manuscript and making helpful comments that have improved it considerably. And a particular thanks to Tannis Calder for her many constructive contributions to the work of Imaginative Education and for examples and ideas. I am especially grateful to Gillian Judson, who read the whole thing, and some bits twice, and one chapter three times, and helped me avoid some bad ideas and bad writing, and made other very useful suggestions for improvement, and also to Mark Fettes, who made a number of insightful suggestions that have significantly improved the manuscript. Frank Baumann, IERG stalwart, Bob Dunston, superintendent of Corbett School District, and Marc Heller, principal of Greenville School, Scarsdale, NY, and Tim Wadington, SFU Ph.D. student, saved me from a number of errors, and Howard Gardner, again, saved me from more, as well as making a number of most helpful suggestions. The errors and inadequacies that persist even after all this generous help are due solely to my many and scarlet academic sins.

During the writing of this book I was the grateful beneficiary of a research grant from the Social Sciences and Humanities Research Council of Canada. I am also grateful to the editors of *Teachers College Record* for permission to use in chapter 2 of this book material that appeared first as "Why Education Is So Difficult and Contentious" in *Teachers College Record* Vol. 103, No. 6, pp. 923–941.

INTRODUCTION

In this modestly titled book I offer, in the first part, an account of why education remains a contentious activity and why the school has been a largely unsatisfactory institution, and I also explain why education — one of the more important human activities — is apparently of so little interest to most intellectuals today. Second, I offer a new way of thinking about education that can resolve many of the problems identified in the first part, and, third, I describe how this new kind of education can replace current forms of schooling.

Chapter 1 sets the context for this exploration of educational problems and cures by looking at the schools of today from two and a half thousand years in the past and two and a half thousand years in the future. In the next chapter I untangle some roots of the knotted idea of education that currently drives our schools and shapes what goes on in them. I expose these roots of our problem and incidentally, to add to the mix of metaphors, explain why the many remedies thrust upon us simply miss the point: solutions and problems pass one another by. Having identified the source of error, I show in the rest of the book how we might go about fixing it. In chapter 3 I describe an alternative and workable idea of education, one that captures what I think most readers will acknowledge is what they really mean by education even if they haven't put it this way. The rest of the book is about how we can get from here to there. The "history" of education from 2010 to 2060 is just a device for showing the practicality of the alternative idea.

This will perhaps occasionally seem a somewhat polemical book, though I may be in danger of taking the fun out of it by saying that it is not aimed at any of the usual targets of educational polemics today. I will not be railing against incompetent teachers, or ignorant school administrators, or malicious and simple-minded politicians and business people, or anti-intellectual progressivists, or elitist and pigheaded traditionalists, or even nutty professors of education. Indeed, I work with the assumption that teachers on the whole are a remarkably dedicated and skilled group of professionals, that educational administrators in my experience work long hours with compassion and concern for the best education of the children in their care, that politicians and business people are also commonly parents and make demands on schools that seem to me generally reasonable, that progressivist educators have been responsible for some of the most important and humane movements in modern schooling and are concerned that children learn what is important about their world, that traditionalist educators are also humane and look to make schools more effective institutions for the welfare of children. That's a rather self-righteous and Panglossian way of putting it, perhaps, but I think the current polemics from teachers against politicians, from progressivists against traditionalists, and vice versa, from business people against school administrators, and vice versa, are examples of flailing at the plague but hitting out at the wrong targets. These polemics are, as a result, generally enervating and fruitless for improving education. We share a frustration but do no good battling each other. My aim in this book is to clarify the target we should jointly be aiming at.

The villain is a bad idea. I want to show what the bad idea is and where it came from and what we can do about it. When we see students unable to read or write very well or see our country's educational failures compared with some other country's relative successes, despite the money we spend, it is easy to look for a scapegoat in some particular group. It is less easy to accept that our fundamental problem in education is theoretical, and that improved and more effective work by all the groups in education will not solve our problem if we have a confusion at the root of the system; running faster with improved style will not help us if we are going in the wrong direction. We behave as we do, design schools of the kinds we have, as a result of the ideas we hold. If we want to improve our schools, it is with the abstract and awkward realm of ideas that we must begin.

Charles A. Beard observed that "the world is largely ruled by ideas, true and false" (1932, p. ix). He went on to quote a "British wit" to the effect that "the power which a concept wields over human life is nicely proportioned to the degree of error in it" (p. ix). We needn't give in to such cynicism, of course, but the witty point pricks because it sometimes seems only too true.

FROM A MAJOR PROBLEM TOWARD A SOLUTION

one

PAST, PRESENT, AND FUTURE SCHOOLS

Imagine you are an Athenian man standing among a group of your fellow citizens about two and a half thousand years ago. Ahead of you, and slightly raised, is a stone altar, beside which wood burns and crackles in a shallow pit. Smoke is rising from a hole in the altar at the end farthest from the pit. A meticulously groomed heifer is being led toward the altar by two men whom you know. It kicks and moos, startled by the fire and the silent crowd, but is forced up the steps. The priestess raises her arms, praises the wisdom of the goddess Athena, and asks her to accept this pure sacrifice and to enjoy the rich smell of its burning meat. The blade of a long knife flashes down into the neck of the heifer. There is a momentary squeal, then silence as its legs give way. The animal is expertly butchered. Its entrails are scooped into long bowls and placed before the priestess on the altar while the carcass is tossed into the burning pit. The priestess pours a cup of wine onto the hissing sacrifice.

As the carcass continues to sizzle, you and your fellow citizens stand silent and tense, watching the priestess swiftly cut away the liver and tip the remaining entrails into the smoking hole in the side of the altar. They add pungently to the smell that most delights the gods. The priestess dissects efficiently and all eyes watch her intently. After a few endless minutes, her bloodied hands hold up pieces of liver. She shouts that it is unspotted, that the goddess Athena is pleased with the sacrifice, and that Athena guarantees success in battle against the Corinthians. A great shout goes up. The goddess has supported those who proposed war and rejection of the peace treaty some had favored.

Later, when the burned meat that Athena most savors is cut away, and after the priestess's portion is set aside, you and your companions receive a small share of the heifer's meat. If, as you enjoy eating it with a bowl of wine around a table with your friends, you suggested to them that cutting up an animal and examining its entrails was not a

3

particularly good way of making foreign policy, you would, of course, be considered crazy. If you persisted in saying that the ceremony you had just been through seemed an unlikely best procedure for running the state, and argued that the condition of heifers' livers had nothing to do with the wisdom or otherwise of going to war, you would be faced with the incredulity of your audience and then perhaps with their hostility. They would likely respond to you patronizingly with their own commonsense arguments.

How else, they would say, do you propose to discover the will of the goddess? The priestess is highly trained, with many years of skilled experience in discovering and interpreting the data. She has a Ph.D. in haruspication from rocky Chios; it is a complex and refined science and provides the most effective methodology for reaching the best political and social decisions. The liver of heifers is known to be the most reliable source of relevant information.

The problem with trying to continue this argument, of course, is that those you wish to argue with take as beyond question precisely what you want to question. They consider themselves commonsense realists because they are intimately familiar with how things are and how they work. If you press your case, the kinder among the group will smile at each other and, when you aren't looking, tap their heads to indicate you are an echinas and hypotrachelion short of a column, or not the sharpest adze in the toolshed.

Now imagine that you are a historian two and a half thousand years in the future. Your special area of study is the distant period between the mid-nineteenth century and the mid-twenty-first century, and you are composing a thesis about a peculiar institution found in every modern society of that ancient time. The school existed as a central institution of what were then considered modern states for just over two hundred years, beginning roughly in the mid-nineteenth century. You are trying to explain, in a clearer way than anyone before you, how such an institution could have come into being in the first place and could have survived so long—despite people at the time constantly complaining about its ineffectiveness.

Your thesis is that twentieth-century people, even though they conducted endless inquiries and commissions and task forces into schools' ineffectiveness, simply failed to identify the fundamental problem. Most reformers were intent on insisting that some particular changes would make the system, finally, more effective. They seemed unable to recognize that the real problem lay in what they so took for granted that they never questioned it. You are thinking of preceding your thesis with a quotation from Ludwig Wittgenstein, a philosopher contemporary with the schools of your research: "One must uncover the source of error otherwise hearing the truth won't help us." A part of your difficulty in composing your argument is that those who will view it, spread across eight star systems, find it incomprehensible that anyone could ever have believed such an institution provided a sensible way to educate children. You recognize the size of your explanatory problem this morning in particular because last night over dinner you tried to outline your thesis to your children and husband.

Your husband knows something about these ancient schools, and he asked how they came into being in the first place. You began by talking about *skhōle*, which meant for the ancient Greeks the suitable use of leisure in cultural activities — particularly literature, music, and gymnastics, with some study of mathematics, cosmology, geography, and the natural world in general. You also mentioned in passing that many of these cultured ancient Greeks believed that state policy should be decided by cutting up animals and inspecting their entrails. Your children looked up from their plates with some amazement. *Skhōle* over time became the word used for the place in which instruction of the young for the proper use of their leisure occurred.

One problem for the later schools you were studying was built in from this earliest time, you explained; this was the belief that learning certain kinds of knowledge made you a more virtuous person. So, learning advanced geometry, say, didn't just mean you knew more geometry than an uneducated person, but that your mind had been made superior in some way. And having a mind made superior by much knowledge enabled you to be a better citizen and better person in general. Such an idea persisted for a long time in those countries which drew on Greek ideas about education, encouraging those who were schooled in privileged forms of knowledge to think of the uneducated classes of their own country as ignorant, boorish, and brutish, and to see people from societies that did not even use writing and had no literate stores of knowledge as primitive or savage.

Your youngest pointed out that these Greeks were a long time before the kind of school you were studying. You explained that schools of many kinds — as places where some children received instruction in how best to use their leisure, and so become superior people — were to be found for centuries. The great events that brought about the kind of school you were studying included the industrial revolution and the agricultural revolution. These and their associated changes led to increasingly powerful centralized states, and also to mechanized war that required huge armies. States needed increasingly to control the lives, and minds, of their populations. One of the main institutions for controlling populations was the school. A new kind of school was invented, grafted rather clumsily onto the Greek kind.

The older school had been a place where the male children of the wealthy learned to use their leisure, whereas the new school was a place to which all children had to go in order to be equipped for productive work, for emotional commitment to the state and its values, and for whatever remnants of the old ideas of cultural and personal development their social backgrounds might be able to support.

Calling the new institutions "schools" helped to disguise their important differences from the older *skhōle*-inspired institutions. The illusion of continuity was further disguised because a number of people hoped the new schools would do for all children what the older schools did for the privileged few. And the old and new institutions shared enough features to justify seeing the new schools as simply a state-led expansion of the older schools; literacy, mathematics, and history, for example, were taught in both, specialized teachers dealt with groups of children, and so on.

You tried to explain how nearly everything anyone might want to do to or for children became the new schools' job. The young of each country became captives within specially designed buildings, sitting more or less docilely in age sets, available for whatever the state or influential interest groups wanted to try. And all kinds of things were tried. Everyone wanted the best for the children; it's just that ideas about what was best were often quite different. So some people still believed that certain forms of knowledge would make children more virtuous, others didn't; some wanted to teach them to accept certain beliefs and values, and others wanted to teach them to be critical of the beliefs and values foisted onto them; some wanted them to follow a careful curriculum toward disciplined knowledge, and others wanted them to explore the world of knowledge for themselves, following their own interests; some wanted to teach the practical skills that would enable the children to get good jobs after school, and others wanted them to concentrate on opening their minds to the arts; most people wanted all of these ideas to be successfully implemented by the school.

But, your oldest child interrupted, why did such a confused institution last so long, especially if people were always arguing about it and complaining that it was generally ineffective? You explained that most people — like the ancient Greeks deciding policy from entrails — just took for granted the institutions they found around them. They considered such institutions to be almost like a part of the natural world; they wouldn't question whether trees should be around or could be improved, and similarly they just took the school for granted.

While some people argued endlessly and bitterly about the school, nearly everyone assumed that some particular reform would fix it. And even after pretty well every reform imaginable had been tried and failed to solve the problems, people just concluded that there would always be *tensions* among the different ideas people had for what the school should be and do. So it staggered forward year by year, with people heroically doing their best to make it work — even though there was a lot of vagueness, confusion, and argument about what it would look like if it were working properly.

Well, let us leave our ancient Greeks eating their roasted heifer, excited and anxious at the prospect of war, and our historian preparing for her morning's work, feeling the warmth of distant Sirius rising and obliterating the sight of the more distant moons currently in the sky. I have dragged you through these past and future scenarios—if you're still with me—to suggest, perhaps overdramatically, that our problems with the school are more fundamental than people today generally believe. To read most books about education, you would get the idea that some particular reform—more attention to "the basics," more freedom for children's exploration, voucher systems and market disciplines, greater use of technology, and so on—would make the school work satisfactorily. I will show that the problem with our modern idea of the school is not fixable by the array of remedies currently on offer. The problem lies elsewhere, and fixing it requires of us the tougher task of rethinking the idea of education we have inherited from ancient and more modern Europe and its tangled history.

two

Beginning with "the abstract and awkward realm of ideas" might not sound so bad. But it can be onerous to think about ideas because they are the things we think *with*. The difficulty is due to our minds being both a part of the world while also being our means of viewing the world—a notoriously problematic duality, which people keep "solving" for us though somehow leaving us with the problem. Our ideas serve us like lenses that greatly affect what we see. Mostly we take our idea-lenses for granted and assume we see reality directly. We don't, of course, and it is useful now and then to try to reflect on our ideas—using other ideas, inescapably. Most people today use three big ideas when they think about education. I'll call them socialization, Plato's academic idea, and Rousseau's developmental idea. The combination of these ideas governs what we do in schools, and what we do to children in the name of education.

Part of our problem with education is that most people combine the three ideas differently—and consequently their idea-lenses disclose to them different educational "realities." Further difficulties are created because each idea is flawed, and each is also significantly incompatible with the other two. I will begin by unraveling our general conception of education into its three main constituent ideas, showing their flaws and then how each tends to undercut the other two thus undermining the effectiveness of our educational institutions.

Bertrand Russell recognized that our current idea of education involves these three distinctive component ideas, each of which leads toward a distinctive aim for schools (1926, ch. 2). He assumed that the solution to the problem of having varied aims was a matter of balancing them properly—though, of course, what constitutes "properly" is what people have been arguing about for a century and a half. More incisively, Zvi Lamm identified the three ideas—which he called socialization, acculturation, and individuation—as incompatible (1976).

9

He showed how each idea was linked to a distinctive purpose of instruction — "training the young for social roles, initiating them into a culture, supporting their self-actualization" (p. 56). He also showed in detail how each undercuts the other two.

But we carry on the educational enterprise assuming that these three aims are compatible, or that their conflicts can be managed if we are sensible in allotting appropriate time and resources to each. In this chapter, though, I want to argue something more radical, echoing Lamm's insight. Consider, as a rough analogy to what I mean, this situation that Arundhati Roy describes in *The Cost of Living* (1999):

> The thing about multipurpose dams like the Sardor Sarovar is that their "purposes" (irrigation, power production, and flood control) conflict with one another. Irrigation uses up the water you need to produce power. Flood control requires you to keep the reservoir empty during the monsoon months to deal with an anticipated surfeit of water. And if there is no surfeit, you are left with an empty dam. And this defeats the purpose of irrigation which is to store the monsoon water. It is like the conundrum of trying to ford a river with a fox, a chicken and a bag of grain.

One shouldn't push such an analogy very far. My purpose in using it is just to indicate that having three fine purposes for an enterprise need not mean that all may be achievable together in the one institution. I'll show why we might reasonably consider the school as having a problem not unlike the multipurpose dams Roy describes. And, of course, you may respond, schools are obviously nothing like as inefficient as such dams after all. But consider the astonishing proportion of the population of Western societies that is functionally illiterate. And most of those who can read rarely read more than formula fiction or self-help books or magazines that rely more on pictures than text. The market in the USA for "literary fiction" or "serious nonfiction" is tiny: a best seller in those categories sells 10,000 copies, in a population approaching 300,000,000. So an institution to which children are compelled to go for more than ten years, whose avowed aim is their education, seems able to generate only the tiniest trickle of interest in the glories of the world's finest literature. I don't mean to suggest that reading "high culture" texts is the crucial mark of educational success — we'll come to that later — but rather that no one's aim for schooling is the degree of illiteracy and semiliteracy that is currently so common. Unlike the purposes of a dam, any one of which could be implemented adequately, each of education's constituent ideas has problems of its own, even before it comes into conflict with the others. The flaws in each of the foundational ideas have already been pointed out, one way or another, usually by proponents of one of the ideas trying to undercut the value of the others. Educational practice in the twentieth century generally went forward under the assumption that the flaws in each idea would be compensated for by the other ideas — that is, three wrong ideas would make a right idea. Alas, it doesn't work, and hasn't worked, that way.

Socialization Is a Great Idea for Hunter-Gatherers

For the educator today, this first great educational idea we have inherited comes as a good-news, bad-news, worse-news, and really-bad-news scenario.

I suppose our educational troubles began around a quarter of a million years ago when our hominid ancestors ran into an evolutionary snag. Around that time, it seems, hominid brains were increasing in size quite rapidly. The snag was the limit to which the size of the female pelvis could be increased to enable women to give birth to these larger-brained babies while also allowing women to walk efficiently. The remarkable evolutionary solution was for babies to be born with immature brains, which then grow mostly outside the womb. So we are today born with brains of around 350 cc, much the same as our chimpanzee cousins. Between birth and adulthood, chimpanzee brains grow about a further 100 cc whereas human brains typically grow well over another 1,000 cc, with most of that additional growth occurring by age four or five. This peculiarity of human brains and human childhood created the need for the extended care and instruction that has become a part of what we mean by education.

Along with the larger brains came language, and language was used prominently to tell stories (Donald, 1991, ch. 7). The most important stories were designed to create for their hearers a conceptual image of what we may call the meaning of life. They gave to the young, and reinforced for older people, images of who "we" are and what we are doing here—in this forest, on this plain, by this seashore, among these hills, alongside these animals, under these stars—and where we are going next. The stories typically told about gods or sacred ancestors who warranted the norms and values that constituted the culture of the particular hunter-gatherer society. The good news is that the techniques invented in hunter-gatherer society to create a homogeneous image of a society, to sanction individual roles within it, and to explain the cosmos in which the drama of our lives is played out, have worked with great success for countless generations. The continuing good news is that the procedures we have inherited from ancient oral cultures remain today wonderfully effective in socializing our young.

For example, we still deploy stories to shape children's understanding and interpretation of experience. Because we do not use traditional myth stories in sacred contexts, we can easily fail to recognize how this ancient technique is ubiquitously used in modern societies to communicate and reinforce who "we" are, what "we" believe, and how "we" should behave. While religious stories are perhaps the most obvious surviving examples, they jostle, and sometimes compete, with a huge variety of more informal stories—jokes and "urban myths," family stories that reinforce certain norms and values (Rosenbluth, 1990), proverbial sayings and warnings echoed from well-known stories, simplified national histories, accounts of office politics, conventional plots of movies and TV shows, and so on. The story is particularly important among the socializing techniques we have inherited because it orients the emotions of the hearers and so more powerfully shapes their commitments to the values and norms coded within it (Egan, 1988).

The bad news is that our evolution equipped us to live in small, stable, hunter-gatherer societies. We are Pleistocene people, but our languaged brains have created massive, multicultural, technologically sophisticated, and rapidly changing societies for us to live in. Now that's not so bad in itself, as our brains can adapt to a huge range of social conditions. The bad news is tied to that ingenious evolutionary adaptation that led to the extended growth of our brains outside the womb. One result of this development—wonderfully efficient for hunter-gatherer tribes—is that in our early years, we learn effortlessly a language, a concept of our society and its norms and values, and conceptions of the meaning of life, the universe, and everything. We are equipped, that is, to orient ourselves conceptually very early and quickly. Whatever children learn from the stories they are first told becomes quickly fixed and serves as a template for future learning. This rapid and deeply etched early learning served hunter-gatherer societies so well because their stability and solidarity were sustained by their members all sharing an unquestioned and homogeneous worldview or ideology.

If one were to try to explain human conceptual development, it would be tempting to say that evolution equipped us with two kinds of learning. There is, first, that largely effortless learning of our early years, which we use to pick up a language and those images of our society and the cosmos. It seems to work a bit like cement or plaster-of-Paris; at first it is enormously flexible, able to adapt to widely varied external constraints, and then gradually it sets and becomes rigid. It also seems to be focused on very specific objects—like language or social behavior. The second kind of learning remains flexible throughout our lives and is a kind of all-purpose utility, but it is more laborious and slow. The difference between the two is often said to be evident in the efficiency with which we learn a language and adapt to social customs in our early years, in contrast with the relative difficulty and inefficiency with which we learn a new language and adapt to new social customs later in life.

Jerry Fodor suggests we might see the mind as having a set of input systems and a somewhat distinct central processor (1983). The input systems are relatively specific to particular parts of the normal brain; they are focused on such things as touch, hearing, seeing, and language. They are fast and "stupid"—we can't fail to hear nor fail to learn a language in normal conditions. The central processor is "smart" and is slow and general in both brain location and operations. This allows very fast responses to some things by the "stupid" brain systems and contemplation and analysis by the other. Fodor notes that "it is, no doubt, important to attend to the eternally beautiful and true. But it is more important not to be eaten" (1985, p. 4).

Well, we might wisely be cautious in inferring such a sharp distinction in kinds of learning as we are still unsure about the underlying cognitive reality such distinctions refer to. But for now the distinction helps to clarify the bad news that comes along with inheriting the idea of socialization *as a part of education*.

Early on, socialization relies heavily on the "stupid" kind of learning and the commitments it forms. If told that the earth is a flat disk that rests on the back of a turtle, nearly everyone will believe this and see the earth in terms of this belief. (An earthquake? The turtle shifted.) If told that it is a huge ball that turns on its axis at high speed while also traveling unimaginably fast around the sun, people will believe this. The cementlike learning of our early years can accommodate almost anything, then it fixes and becomes almost immovable. The other, general-purpose learning capacity can, of course, accumulate knowledge that contradicts the first-formed beliefs, and we know that we can, as a result, change our earlier beliefs and commitments. We also know that this is rare and difficult for most people. The stories we are first told, and the other techniques of socialization deployed early, pretty well fix the values people hold until their death. They become the things people think with, not the things they think about.

The bad news, then — to put it crudely — is that we live in a world that requires flexibility in adapting to changing norms, beliefs, and values, but evolution has equipped us to be socialized in a manner that creates rigidity and commitment to a particular set of quickly outdated norms, beliefs, and values. Today, for most children in the West, literacy, critical thinking, tolerance for others, and so on, form part of the set of "norms, beliefs, and values" they take on board during early socialization. What's the bad news in this? We'll come later to the differences between a socialized literacy, critical thinking, and tolerance and their educational forms. Sometimes the differences may appear subtle in description on the page, but they are usually gross in practice. Socialization is a process determined by the criterion of current social needs and values. Society provides a template according to which the variety of human possibilities is limited, constrained, and homogenized to what is currently required, or to what a reasonable projection of future social needs suggests will be required. The bad news is tied to the limits on human possibilities that society's needs impose. And, yes, we can all imagine an ideal society that would encourage endless exploration of possibilities. The problem for socialization as a component of education is not so much that we have never had, do not now have, and likely never will have such a society, but that its homogenizing requirements will always be at odds with the ambitions of our imaginations. For now, though, instead of considering socialization in terms of some ideal conception of society shaping its citizens for ideal lives, let us think of it in terms of the everyday demands made on the school by the government, the business sector, and interest groups, each of which wants to shape children for their purposes. This is, after all, the reason governments are in the business of schooling.

The worse news, which follows from the bad news, is that if socialization is really successful, the result is someone who is indoctrinated. Now we tend to be very acute at recognizing the ways in which "others" indoctrinate their children, but we are largely oblivious to the forms of indoctrination we deploy ourselves; "they" indoctrinate, "we" educate. Of course, they think we indoctrinate and they educate — but that's only because they have been indoctrinated to think so. Five-year-olds in Tokyo, Teheran, Baghdad, St. Petersburg, Winnipeg, San Francisco, Madang, and so on, across the disk on the turtle's back, have already learned complex sets of beliefs and patterns of behavior whose validity they will never seriously question. We label as indoctrination those that are most in conflict with our own.

This leads to a conundrum. "We" distinguish indoctrination from education by the openness of inquiry the educator encourages about the values taught, whereas the indoctrinators teach "their" values as unquestionable truths. But we do not typically encourage our children to question the value of our kind of "openness of inquiry" — we teach its value as an unquestionable truth. We'll return to this after considering the really bad news, which results from one of the effects on our thinking that comes along with language.

Thinking in language leads us to recognize and name things as distinct from all other things — x is what not-x is not, goes the logic. Whether this results from the hard-wiring of our brains or from the way language shapes our consciousness, we have a powerful tendency to construct our conceptual grasp on the world in terms of opposites. Our sense of "good" is tied to our sense of "bad," big to little, brave to cowardly, safe to dangerous, and so on; there sometimes seems to be no "yes" without its "no," no x without its −x. ("The real world is continuous, but our inner world of features is discrete because features elicit a binary yes/no response" [Stewart and Cohen, 1997, p. 168].)

When hunter-gatherers distinguished who "we" are, the distinction was with who "they" were. This characteristic of socialization we have also inherited. For the hunter-gatherers, "we" are recognized faces and are treated as friends; "they" are unknown, potential enemies, and one must be prepared to kill them before they kill "us." As Jared Diamond puts it: "With the rise of chiefdoms around 7,500 years ago, people had to learn, for the first time in history, how to encounter strangers regularly without attempting to kill them" (1997, p. 273).

Socialization today not only fits us to a particular social group but also identifies "us" to ourselves as distinct from other groups. Becoming American, or Canadian, or English still involves learning about the distinctive qualities that characterize the excellence of one's nation by contrast with other nations which lack those qualities. Even within a country, we will identify ourselves again in contrast with others; so we conservatives or liberals identify ourselves in some degree by contrast with those liberals or conservatives.

Our seemingly inescapable tendency to oppositional thinking produces a horrible result when it works in socializing. It sets people against each other, to a greater or lesser degree. The trick, as Richard Rorty suggests, is to increase the range of people we include as "we," thus widening our solidarity with others (1989). But our history suggests that we then will begin to make divisions within the group. Even the local stamp club or choir develops factions with bewildering ease. For much of the time, in groups, we are a contentious animal. Now this is all a bit odd, as we can't give up socializing our children despite these problems. Even if socialization does require some degree of indoctrination, some homogenizing, some degree of fixing certain beliefs and values beyond the easy reach of rational reflection, as long as those beliefs and values are decent, shouldn't we just go along with the process? If our values include tolerance and a positive attitude to other races and cultures, won't socialization that fixes these values firmly prepare our children well for these complex multicultural societies we have made? If the indoctrination part of socializing discourages our children from questioning the value of tolerance, can that be so bad?

Socialization as an educational ideal worked well in hunter-gatherer tribes. But today we can't easily avoid squirming a little about the dilemma it creates for us. On the one hand, we have to allow considerable scope for socialization to occur unimpeded in order for our children to become at home in our society, but on the other hand, we are committed to rationality in our everyday affairs, and our rationality is affronted by the homogenizing and indoctrinatory elements in successful socialization. Also, to fail to socialize adequately produces alienation. Our general solution to the dilemma has been to recognize that single-minded socialization — à la the Hitler Youth — is unacceptable, and that we need, double-mindedly, to give rational reflection a large role in the process. And that's where we try to plug Plato in.

The Academic Ideal and Asses Loaded with Books

The next really big development in human intellectual culture after the development of language was the invention of literacy. The spread of literacy, and the spread of knowledge stored in literate codes, required the invention of the school to initiate children into the new forms of coded knowledge. Professional initiators were also required, as it was no longer enough to work alongside your parents or relatives to learn the skills adulthood would require of you. While literacy may be counted as one of the most productive of human inventions, transforming our conditions of life and the conditions of our minds like no other, for the poor educationalist it is the source of another huge set of problems. Clearly literacy has been in general a good-news scenario, but it also carries for the educator some bad news, some worse news, and some really bad news.

The good news is easy to see. Literacy has allowed generations of people to record their knowledge and experience. Further generations can compare that recorded knowledge with what they can see or discover themselves, and they can leave a more accurate record; they can compare others' experience with their own, enlarging and enriching their experience in consequence. Today we have stored vast amounts of knowledge in written records, and we have access to a vast array of varied human experience; at least, it seems vast to us today. Once decoded, these written records enable our minds to transcend our own time, place, and circumstances.

Eric Havelock argued that Plato's great achievement was to work out how to think once alphabetic literacy became common (1963, 1982, 1986). The result is both described and, if you'll excuse the term, paradigmatically exemplified in Plato's dialogues. When the best accumulated knowledge coded in writing is learned, Plato taught, it transforms the minds of the learners and enables them to understand the world more accurately and truly.

The bad news in this for today's educators is that they have to work out what, of the vast accumulation available, is the best knowledge for children to learn. Herbert Spencer was confident that his answer to his question "What knowledge is of most worth?" was unassailable. But, of course, everyone assailed it. Is the best knowledge that of the "timeless classics," "the best that has been thought and said," as Matthew Arnold claimed, or of urgent social conditions, or of economically productive skills? Or should children's own interests determine their curricula, or should our school curriculum be a smorgasbord of all the above laid out by committees of "stakeholders," or should we have different curricula for different people, or a common or core curriculum for all, or what? The bad news is not so much that we don't know the answer in any generally agreed way, but we don't seem able to agree on how we might go about reaching an agreed answer. In the absence of any convincing theoretical grasp on the question, it is left to political power — to the committees of "stakeholders" laying out the smorgasbord — to answer. This might be a good solution if we think of education simply as socializing, but it is a lousy solution if we think education has something to do with that ideal Plato articulated for enabling us to understand the world and transcend the (socialized) conventions of our time and place.

The worse news is that, whatever the knowledge some group decides is worthiest for inclusion in our curricula, most students find literacy such a barrier that they will be unable to access that knowledge anyway. It ought to be easy to teach children to read and write. The great cultural breakthrough made by the invention of the Greek alphabet — from which all modern alphabets are derived — democratized, one might say, reading and writing. One had to learn only twenty or so symbols that could be combined to approximate the sounds of oral language. But becoming literate has never been as easy as it seems it ought to be. Most people find reading a lot of text very difficult, and when not compelled to do so, they don't. When it comes to writing, most people find it almost impossible to compose a coherent piece of prose that can express what they think with economy, clarity, and elegance. A note or e-mail message in dull conventional terms is as much as the majority can manage, despite years and years of expensive teaching.

For most children, school disrupts and significantly destroys the orality of their early years by insistently trying to teach literacy and the knowledge coded in literate forms. For most children, school fails to provide access to the glories of literacy and to literacy's transcendent culture. A complaint of aboriginal people on the west coast of Canada who had been compelled to send their children to residential schools was that "they taught them to read and made them stupid." The schools disrupted and significantly destroyed the children's native oral culture, and in its place were able to put only a crude and debased literacy. This is analogous to what we do to most children in schools.

The really bad news is that there isn't any knowledge stored in literacy, in all our libraries and databases. What we can store are symbols that are a cue to knowledge. People can read the symbols and not understand the knowledge, or partially understand it, or have only a vague sense of what it means. This happens in schools to such an extent that we expect it and grade children by the degree of understanding we think they have achieved.

The problem here is that knowledge exists only in living human tissue, and the literacy codes we use for storage are cues that need to go through a complex transformation before they can be brought to life again in another mind. Many educationalists, and even more non-educationalists, confuse the codes with knowledge. They assume that if the students internalize the codes they will have the knowledge. Alas, not so. We can relatively easily compel or persuade or seduce people into internalizing literate codes, so they can pass exams and seem knowledgeable. This kind of learning has been the bane of insightful educators down the centuries. What it produces is not knowledgeable people but, as Michel de Montaigne put it, asses loaded with books. In a characteristic outburst, J.-J. Rousseau — that bookish man who described how his own early reading set his mind afire — famously wrote: "I hate books: they only teach one to talk about what one does not know" (1762/1979, p. 184).

Howard Gardner describes a modern rediscovery of this phenomenon in an experiment involving the most successful science students at leading universities. When given problems based on principles they had learned but in contexts different from those in which they had learned the principles, they typically responded incorrectly in much the same way as a typical unschooled five-year-old (1991, ch. 1). The students drew on the intuitive folk physics they picked up in those early years of effortless learning. Their dozen years of physics in school and university was an insecure accumulation compared with the foundational knowledge of their preschool years. The trouble is that the intuitive folk physics is wholly inadequate to a scientific understanding of the physical world.

We all recognize the difference between genuine knowledge and accumulated codes — we talk of education as against training, wisdom as against "book learning," insight as against literal thinking, and so on. But our schools are not good either at recognizing the difference or, consequently, at promoting the genuine article rather than the counterfeit. And, as usual, Gresham's law applies — debased coin drives out good. T. S. Eliot's "Where is the knowledge we have lost in information?" cannot be answered if one doesn't recognize a difference. Nearly all our techniques of assessing students' achievement deal only with the latter, and so teachers focus on the information at the expense of living knowledge and imaginative engagement with it, and the system favors and advances those students who are efficient in dealing with information and who "can solve problems as problems divorced from human sense" (Donaldson, 1978, p. 76). We hope, of course, that there is a correlation between this most prized schooling skill and being sensible and knowledgeable, but it's only a hope.

The problem Gardner writes about is the same Montaigne complained of. In Montaigne's day, the richness and abundance of understanding that should have come to all students from literacy through an education in the classics had too often descended into dry pedantry. The nineteenth-century reformers saw the dry pedantry and assumed it was the classical curriculum that caused it. ("Anyone who has passed through the regular gradations of a classical education, and is not made a fool by it, may consider himself as having had a very narrow escape" [Hazlitt, 1826/1951, p. 147].) So in its place they created a more "relevant" curriculum, and their progressive successors through the twentieth century have remained puzzled that it has produced similar, and even worse, results — not so much pedantry but ignorance so extensive that there has been nothing much to be pedantic about.

The really bad news, then, is that some kind of magic (or technique we aren't reliably good at replicating) is required to bring back to new life in a new mind the desiccated written codes in which knowledge was stored by some other, perhaps long-dead, human mind. But even if we can manage the magic, I'm afraid there is even worse news than the really bad news. That is, even at its best, Plato's academic ideal can't deliver on its promises.

Plato describes an educational program that will carry the mind from the confusions and illusions of the folk physics, folk psychology, and folk sociology learned effortlessly in our early years, through a curriculum of disciplined knowledge, to an understanding of the true nature of things. It is a program that requires the sacrifice of easy pleasures and the deployment of our laborious general-learning capacity to remake all our early false knowledge, converting our minds always toward rationality and truth and away from the seductions of beliefs and myths. We are to climb beyond personal interest in looking at the world and so see it objectively. It is not clear that Plato's, or anyone's, curriculum can deliver these benefits. It is not clear that the products of high literacy include justice, objectivity, and truth. Plato believed these were the fruits of his educational program and justified the austere discipline necessary to gather them. It is probably a better educational idea than anyone before or since has had, but it is not adequate. The worst news, then, is that the academic ideal of education is designed to achieve a kind of understanding it simply can't deliver.

The Idea of Development

I linked the two previous educational ideas/ideals with, first, the development of language and, second, the invention of literacy. For the sake of symmetry, it would be nice to link this third educational idea with the invention of printing and with the new learning and "Enlightenment" it seemed to many in Europe to promise. Even if the causal connection is not quite so easily made, the printing press was certainly importantly complicit in those intellectual changes which included the radical rethinking of the nature of education in the work of John Locke (1632–1704), Etienne Bannot de Condillac (1715–1780), and, crucially, Jean-Jacques Rousseau (1712–1778).

Their reconceiving of education seems, in retrospect, a part of the new learning most signally represented in the *Philosophiæ Naturalis Principia Mathematica* (Mathematical Principles of Natural Philosophy; 1687) by Isaac Newton (1642–1727). This work looked like the triumphant confirmation of the Enlightenment belief that scientific observation of nature would produce data that could, by the application of reason, disclose the laws according to which the whole cosmos worked. Rousseau argued that human beings also have a nature and a natural process of development that could be disclosed by careful observation aided by reason. As we can observe the body's regular pattern of development from birth to old age, so we can, with more difficulty perhaps, observe the mind's regular pattern of development. Education was reconceived as the activity of supporting the fullest achievement of the natural process of mental development.

An implication of this revolutionary idea — from a man who specialized in such products — was to discount the centrality of preparing for active citizenship as a part of education. Indeed, Rousseau suggested that we face a fundamental conflict between forming the citizen and forming the individual. Individuals are formed by our learning to attend honestly and sensitively to the prompting of our consciences, not by attending to instructions from others, to society's lectures, sermons, and requirements. It is in the depths of our hearts that we discover our real nature and learn to be true to it; that is how we become individuals rather than merely cogs in the engines of society. And while we do have to become citizens, we first and separately have to become our true selves. The proper development of the mind, then, comes from discovering our individual nature and focusing our attention on creating the conditions for its fullest growth, not from learning some approved body of external knowledge.

This idea came as good news for educationalists, but also — you guessed it — there was bad news, worse news, and really bad news that came with it.

The good news was that it promised to solve a problem that Plato's idea left us with. Rousseau acknowledged that Plato (hitherto) had been the greatest educational thinker. Plato had recognized how knowledge shaped the mind and how particular kinds of abstract knowledge, and the disciplines they required, shaped the mind to understand the world in more adequate and effective ways. But it had become clear that this wasn't enough. The common product of a Platonic education was asses loaded with books, or informed pedantry without imagination, originality, or vigor. Rousseau proposed that the missing element was the knowledge that we could deduce from careful observation of the natural course of development, the different ways we learn at different ages, and the different ways different individuals learn.

So Plato, Rousseau suggests, was right about the importance of knowledge in education, but his insight was of limited value without recognition of the stages at which the young can best learn the various kinds of knowledge and the ways different individuals learn. Plato failed to recognize the mind's autonomous growth, and so his conception of mental development was just a mirror image of his conception of the logic whereby knowledge was elaborated, that is, the mind, to Plato, was an epistemological organ. By understanding the autonomous growth of the mind, Rousseau believed (and seems to have persuaded nearly everyone involved with education today) one could coordinate the logic of knowledge elaboration with the psycho-logic of mental development.

The continuing good news is that educationalists more or less universally now believe that it is important to attend to the nature of the child's learning at particular developmental stages, to support different "learning styles," and to cultivate that range of sensitivities to learners that became a hallmark of progressivism. Once attention to the distinctive psychological development of the child was made central to educationalists' understanding of their task, a number of considerable benefits followed. The first and perhaps still the most important was the recognition that failures to learn the curriculum might be due to faults other than the child's recalcitrance. It might, for example, be due to the method of teaching or the "stage" at which a topic was being taught. This recognition eventually led to relieving children's school lives of the constant fear of violence for failures to learn. It took a long time for this benefit to follow from Locke's and Rousseau's formulation of educational ideas, but we should not underestimate the importance of this humanitarian result of attending to the nature of the learner.

The combination of Plato's idea about knowledge and Rousseau's idea about the mind was launched by Rousseau with the promise of a revolution in learning. Through the twentieth century, each claim by a theorist, most notably Jean Piaget, to having more adequately exposed the developmental process has led to a renewal of the promise of a revolution in learning. The enterprise of psychological research in education that tries to discover the nature of learning, development, motivation, and so forth, has gone forward on the promise — as one of its early prophets put it — of "pedagogical possibilities now undreamed of" (Hall, 1904, II, p. 222).

The bad news is that the revolution in learning has stubbornly refused to occur. It seemed, and still seems to many, that research which discloses increasing knowledge about children's development and learning must lead to, at least, evident improvements in general education. The trouble with promising a revolution in learning is that people expect to see some evidence of it in the learners.

What did become evident was that the commitment to freedom for natural development doesn't take one very far. As an educational idea, it makes it difficult to determine a curriculum and tends to leave the selection of curriculum material open to local prejudice, charismatic enthusiasts, or blind chance. To keen progressivists, however, this doesn't matter that much because the curriculum isn't the point.

We have had a century of fairly intensive experiment in implementing varied forms of the idea we have inherited from Rousseau, and of progressivism's interpretations of it, and of educational psychology's attempts to flesh it out scientifically. It seems fair to observe at this point that something is still missing. Plato's and Rousseau's ideas together are not able to bring about for most children the kind of learning we see in some, and the kind of learning that it doesn't seem unreasonable to expect from hugely expensive schools. After a few centuries of careful observation and one century of intensive research on development, it is hard to see what evident improvements in general education have resulted. The promise of Rousseau's idea has not been delivered. Alas, it hasn't worked.

The worse news is that it can't work. The worse news follows the observation that human beings don't have a nature. Well, that overstates it to underline a point. There are obviously regularities in human mental development, but they are so tied up with our social experience, our culture, and the kinds of intellectual tools we pick up that we can't tell whether the regularities are due to our nature, to our society, to our culture, to our intellectual tools, or what. We can't simply measure the regularities, which turn out to be pretty irregular from person to person anyway, and see through them to our nature, or to some autonomous developmental process. The Russian psychologist Lev Vygotsky pointed this out as a fatal flaw in Piaget's theory in the 1920s, but it is only now, with the generally recognized foundering of Piaget's theory, that the force of Vygotsky's criticism is coming home to many. It puts in mind Gertrude Stein's quip about Oakland — There is no there there — only in this case, it's that there is no nature of mental development there.

The really bad news is that Rousseau put in place for the modern educational world a binary distinction between an autonomously developing mind and an "external" body of knowledge. Once education was thought of in terms of knowledge and mind (content and method, curriculum and instruction), the problem became how to get them back together again. The history of educational thinking in the twentieth century prominently involved a bizarre war between those who were "subject-centered" and those who were "child-centered," between traditionalists and progressivists.

If you begin to think of education as facilitating the ideal development of individuals' minds, you have the problem of dealing with the role knowledge is to perform in this process. Progressivism emphasized the general uselessness of the "traditional" classical curriculum and promoted the value of useful knowledge that responded to current social needs. That is, Rousseau's dichotomy undermined Plato's "epistemological mind," in which the mind grew in direct response to, and in proportion with, the knowledge the individual learned. Because Rousseau's idea became persuasive, the mind is assumed to go through its own autonomous process, given "natural," normal, or spontaneous interactions with its environment, and knowledge is selected for the curriculum based on its social utility. Tatters of the old classical curriculum hang around, partly out of an intuition that there might be something in Plato's idea and partly to satisfy the minority who still want that old-style "ornamental" education. For the core of the new progressive curricula, however, utility trumps transcendence every time — Career and Personal Planning, Drug Education, Economics for Everyday Living, or Computers 101 trump Latin hands down in the competition for limited curriculum time.

Rousseau's dichotomy, adopted by Spencer, Dewey, and pretty well all other progressive educationalists, has given us a century of polemical battles between supporters of "child-centeredness" and supporters of "subject-centeredness." We are, of course, suckers for a neat dichotomy — why else do we go to war? The polemical battles are one result of the really bad news resulting from Rousseau's idea.

Institutions Based on Incompatible Ideas

We obviously haven't inherited these three great educational ideas in the more or less discrete packages described above. We don't, of course, think of our conception of education as a composite but rather as a unitary idea. But those three ideas have become entangled with each other through the centuries and have produced our contemporary schools and curricula and teaching practices.

When we do note differences among the competing demands of these three ideas — when, for example, politicians or business people demand from the schools more relevant social knowledge or work skills or when some neoconservatives demand we concentrate on developing academic knowledge — we say that there are "tensions" among the requirements of the various "stakeholders." The job of the good educational administrator is to balance these tensions, so that the requirements of all the major stakeholders are met to an adequate degree. We have come to live with these "tensions" so long that most see them as inevitable and as a management problem. This is how we disguise confusions from ourselves, conceptually papering over deep fault lines in our thinking.

Each of our three ideas, then, has significant flaws. Well, of course — has been the response since the mid-nineteenth century — that's why we put them together. Judicious application of one or another of the ideas supports or constrains the third; each solves problems created by the others. So the academic idea has been used to provide support for individual development and to put a brake on excessive socialization; socialization has been used to give individual development a sense of direction and to provide a check on the élitism of the academic idea; and individual development has been used to check the excessive intellectualism of the academic idea and to enrich, enlarge, and diversify socialization. Ah, the best of all possible worlds!

To put a slightly less positive spin on it, our three defective ideas prevent each other from doing too much damage. So, we socialize, but we undercut indoctrination by the academic program calling society's values into question and by the commitment to individual development reducing society's claims on any particular individual; we pursue an academic program, but we undercut intellectual élitism by egalitarian pressures from socialization and by attention to other dimensions of individual development; we encourage individual development, but we undercut its fulfillment by the homogenizing pressures of socialization and by the standardizing brought about by a common academic curriculum. Ah, what a wonder of compromise is our modern conception of education!

Can it really be true that our conception of education has three main components, each one of which leads to undesirable results by itself, and which work together only by each one interfering with the adequate implementation of the other two? Surely this is a pessimistic fantasy? Do the schools that have been built on this tripartite conception of education — that is, nearly all modern schools — fail to provide students with an adequate academic education? Well, there has certainly been a chorus of critics who have vociferously argued over the years that typical schooling leaves students woefully ignorant of their cultural heritage. Do schools fail to provide adequate socialization? Certainly critics have constantly complained about students' alienation on the one hand and their common lack of civic values on the other. And do schools fail to provide adequate development of individual students' potential? We do still hear loud criticism about the irrelevance of much schooling to students' individual needs.

Well, of course there are such criticisms, you might reasonably point out. This is a democracy, after all. Even optimists don't expect perfect implementation of all three ideas. The great success of our education system is to have achieved a somewhat shifting balance among three distinct aims. Schools provide an exposure to academic material for all students, and clearly allow some to excel in academic work; they socialize all students in a basic way while avoiding fanatical extremes; and they attend to the general development of all children and provide special help to some who clearly need it. Of course there are tensions among the three general educational ideas that drive our schools — successful education is achieved by finding the right community-supported balance.

I have tried to suggest that this commonsense, realistic response, which takes a generally optimistic view of schooling, should be viewed as like the sensible friends' explanation of why cutting up heifers' livers is obviously the best way to decide social-policy issues. So let me try to persuade you to see our schools in a less complacent way — not that *you* see them in a complacent way, but my lugubrious picture of flawed and incompatible foundations is obviously not one that appeals to people daily involved in making the current system work.

Consider this scenario: The government, responding to mounting social dissatisfaction about injustices in the way people's salaries are currently determined, which has led to massive disparities in income, has introduced legislation to radically reorganize how salaries will be allotted in the future. You will continue to do your usual job, but everyone will be required to go to the cinema one evening each week.

After the film is over, you come out into the foyer where there will be rows of single desks. You have to take a seat behind a desk and, on a time signal, begin answering a multiple-choice test about the film you have just seen. You will be asked such questions as the color of the villain's car in the second chase scene, the name of the heroine's dog, the adequacy of the female assassin's motivation, the gist of the alien's speech before it transmogrified, and so on. Your score on the test will determine your salary for the next week. One week later you will see another film and take another test, and your salary will be adjusted for the following week depending on your score. And so on every week for the rest of your working life. Consider for a moment how such tests and their consequence would likely influence your watching movies. At the very least, they would change what was carefree enjoyment into anxiety. You would also spend a lot of effort during the film trying to second-guess the kinds of questions you are likely to be asked, and the focus of your attention would be shifted to fit your expectations of the test.

What does this remind you of? Right. School. The above absurd scenario creates a social institution — with, no doubt, huge testing services and solemn officials and entrepreneurs setting up test-coaching companies — that confuses two conflicting aims. There is no problem with having two aims for an institution, except if the aims are mutually conflicting. If one of our aims for an educational institution is the pursuit of academic knowledge, we will interfere with that in all kinds of destructive ways if we then impose a social-sorting role on the institution and use the results of academic testing to do that social sorting. Also the social-sorting role would be confused because academic prowess — which we are only marginally testing for anyway — is hardly the most important determiner of social value. That is, this kind of undermining by separate and conflicting aims is precisely what we get if we try to make the school an institution that tries both to socialize students and to implement the academic ideal at the same time. The result is that neither is adequately or sensibly achieved, as, in the cinema scenario, neither carefree entertainment nor an appropriate manner of determining salaries is achieved.

Yet we take it for granted that the student who is able to recall at some specific time the provisions of the Treaty of Augsburg and who is more efficient at doing those mathematical problems that involve three and a half men digging a ditch seven feet deep, and so on, should be given better chances to get better jobs that the student who is less good at such tasks. Two things are wrong with this current assumption. First, it is not clear — except that it becomes a self-fulfilling prophecy — that the skills that lead to being successful in school tests coincide with the skills that lead to being successful at the jobs the test success makes available. Second, it *is* clear that using what ought to be the material of historical and mathematical understanding for this social-sorting purpose debases, abuses, and undermines the academic purposes of studying them.

Consider a second scenario: You are fifty-five and have had a successful career as a lawyer. You have a spouse and two successful children. You are a pillar of the community, active in church, community center, and sports activities. But it has recently become disturbingly clear that you will not remain vigorous forever, and that time is closing in. Something in you is unsatisfied, like a distant echo from a life path you somewhere missed taking, like a call from another you who was not realized — but still might be. It is a disturbing call, a distressing echo, which grows louder by the day. Increasingly you feel it is a call from the real you, a call from your buried life; from the you who somehow got lost in all those legal tussles and in the social round and the kids' soccer and ballet and then their colleges and marriages, and now that ghostly you calls to be recognized and brought to life. Well, fortunately, you can enroll in the required government program, ReTRY. ReTRY — an acronym for Realize The Real You — is slickly operated by the country's best and most expensive psychologists. It is mandated by law to assist citizens' psychological adjustment to later middle age. Success in the program is measured by the degree to which people return satisfied to their old routines of life.

Hang on. How can an institution designed to help you find the real you measure success by convincing you that the old you is the real you? Shouldn't you be encouraged to head out yonder to dive in the pearl seas, paint in the South Pacific, swagger the nut-strewn roads, or at least take up kayaking or building a Japanese garden? Socializing draws its criteria from social needs, and it needs to fit you to slots society has available; however, your individual development requires the elaboration of your personal distinctiveness and the fulfillment of your potential as far as possible. Now it is true that being a social animal, we find our fulfillment within society, but we will always find some conflict between society's need to homogenize and constrain and our individual desire for freedom and exploration of our uniqueness. Rousseau argued that "forced to combat nature or the social institutions, one must choose between making a man or a citizen, for one cannot do both at the same time" (1979, p. 39). Rousseau recommended that we focus on individual development entirely for the early years, as one can always become a citizen later, whereas if one is raised to be a citizen, one will never develop one's individuality. I think we might doubt how far Rousseau's Émile would later become an adequate citizen. But we expect our modern schools to manage both successfully.

Socializing strives to homogenize; individual development strives to bring out the uniqueness of each person. Hard to aim for both in the same institution and expect success. They constantly pull in opposite directions — the more you do one, the harder it is to do the other.

Consider a third scenario: It is twenty years in the future, and the government's educational authorities have become convinced that the route to the fullest development of each individual's potential is to design different kinds of schools to support the main styles of learning and kinds of intelligence people deploy. There are ten kinds of schools. Enormously sophisticated testing apparatus and procedures are applied to children to determine which school would most fully develop their particular strengths. Huge amounts of money have been spent on designing the schools, outside and in, to respond to, and stimulate, the needs of the kinds of students they house. The curriculum in each kind of school, however, is identical. The children follow a rigorous academic program designed to carry their minds from the ignorance and confusion of their originally unschooled condition toward a disciplined understanding of their cultural heritage. There are no electives, until university specialization, because the authorities have also been convinced that the only proper aim of education is to empower children's minds with the best material human beings have created, and that is precisely what the disciplined forms of understanding provide. But such a system would surely be self-contradictory. The academic commitment to shaping the mind by teaching disciplined forms of understanding isn't compatible with the belief that the minds of different people can be optimally developed by knowledge chosen to suit their particular style of learning, kind of intelligence, needs, and interests. One cannot have two masters, especially when both mandate different things. We can't construct a coherent educational institution using radically different criteria, one set of criteria driving us centripetally toward a common-core academic curriculum, the other set driving us centrifugally toward diversity and difference based on individual needs. In the one case our criteria are drawn from the nature of knowledge, in the other they are drawn from our sense of the needs of different minds. While in general and abstract terms this might seem surmountable by a bit of clever word work, it is well to consider that the abstractions point to the unrelenting disputes we have witnessed for a century and a half between advocates of traditional and progressivist educational schemes.

But that's precisely what we require of our schools today. We require that they acknowledge, and accommodate as far as possible, different styles of learning and different ends of the process for different people. "Education" for one child may have a quite different character from that attained by another; quite different "potentials" might be developed and each can be an example of successful education. We require also that the academic ideal — which recognizes education only in the degree to which minds are shaped by progress in understanding the range of disciplines — be acknowledged. The result, of course, is not a coherent curriculum, but one that tries to accommodate both conflicting principles. The result, also, is perpetual strife by adherents of the conflicting principles, fighting about which should have greater influence over children's education.

Conclusion

One doesn't want to get too hung up on classificatory schemes; it becomes too easy to see everything in terms of them. A scheme can provide something "good to think with" about the issues it organizes, but then it runs the danger of displacing what it is supposed to help expose. But maybe I can go a little further with this one, without becoming a mad classifier slotting everything into the three categories as though that is all that needs to be said about education. I have obviously simplified educational ideas to fit them into three discrete boxes, and I have ignored the fact that each of the three ideas is far from a simple unitary position. Within each there is a continuum of positions, and there are people who are attracted to bits and pieces of each in various ways. Perhaps the general scheme of this chapter might be seen simply as a heuristic device, enabling better understanding of why education has remained such a contentious business for the past century and a half, and pointing towards the distinct solution of the problem that takes up the rest of this book.

(Mind you, it's worth noting that one does see these ideas fairly explicitly evident in nearly all areas of educational conflict. I came across a discussion of the arguments made in the late nineteenth century when it was proposed to introduce English into the university curriculum. It became clear that the proponents had quite different ideas about what the purpose of this new area of study should be. The competing positions were represented as "literature as an object of knowledge," as "a means to personal growth," and as "a means of social cohesion." The author marveled that the recent arguments about revising the English curriculum in the schools of her country (England) simply repeated exactly the same arguments and positions that had been made more than a century earlier. And those arguments, of course, exactly represent the three main educational ideas I have explored above.)

Each idea seems to commit its adherents to a somewhat different conception of the mind. To the socializer, the mind is largely a social organ, whose realization can occur only within a particular social setting. The educational trick for such a person is to make the society as good as possible so that fitting into it will fulfill individuals as well as possible. But within this position, there is a wide range of viewpoints, from those who consider the present social structures generally satisfactory and who want students educated to fit those structures, to those who want the schools to help reform and transform the society in desirable ways, which in turn will enrich the educational experience. In my general terms this continuum of beliefs all fit within the socializing group *because the criteria of education that dominate their thinking are derived from the current or hoped-for future condition of society.*

To the academic, the mind is largely an epistemological organ; it is made up of the knowledge it has learned. The educational trick for such a person is to make sure students learn as much as possible of those things that have proven over the years most stimulating to the mind. Within this position there is a great variety too, from those who see the "best that has been thought and said" in the stable and reliable classics, to those who consider modern knowledge of the sciences and cutting-edge arts as best able to stimulate the mind appropriately. What makes both ends of this continuum fit within the academic classification is that *their primary criterion for determining the curriculum is to be found in the value of particular kinds of knowledge for enriching the mind.*

To the person most committed to individual development, the mind is largely a psychological organ. The educational trick for this person is to search out whatever seems most likely to stimulate and support the mind's process of development. Within this stance, too, there is a wide variety of positions, from the belief that the main function of the educator is to facilitate students' development by removing obstacles to their free exploration of the world, to the belief that a curriculum should be designed from those features of the world, such as classical music or academic knowledge, which students should be exposed to in order to discover what particular features will most assist their distinct growth. What makes these diverse positions fit under my individual development category is that *they use an image*

35

of the development of the individual student's mind as the determining criterion for what should be done in his or her education.

Well, so much for classifying. But this scheme, I have claimed, can help us see the error at the foundations of the currently dominant idea of education that drives our schools. I have argued that we have inherited three foundational ideas about education. Each one of them has flaws, at least one flaw in each being fatal to its ambition to represent an educational ideal we might reasonably sign on to. And the worse news is that each of the ideas is incompatible with the other two. These warring ideas hovered around the cradle of the state schools, proffering their gifts. The schools eagerly took them all, and so education remains difficult and contentious.

Well, having thought about the ideas we usually think with, where are we? A plausible answer is, in something of a mess. The commonest response to inspecting the foundations of our ideas and finding them inadequate is to turn and carry on with everything much as before. I mean, think of the trouble we would have to go to if we were to conclude that indeed our conception of education is flawed in the way this chapter has argued and that we should do something about it! In general, most people seem to be sustained by institutions not ideas. That the institutions are as they are because of particular ideas seems not to be a matter that concerns most people in the education business. Practical folk just get on with doing the best they can within the institutions that exist. And, of course, without this pragmatic commonsense approach, we would be in a bigger mess.

But what would we have to do if we take ideas seriously, understand how they shape institutions, and conclude that the above argument is generally right? First off, we need a better idea of education than the fractious confusion we currently stumble along with. And where will we find such a thing? Well, we just have to make it up. We might sensibly follow John Dewey's advice: "It is the business of an intelligent theory of education to ascertain the causes for the conflicts that exist and then, instead of taking one side or the other, to indicate a plan of operation proceeding from a level deeper and more inclusive than is represented by the practices and ideas of the contending parties" (1963, p. 5).

I really can't see any likely good return from the continuing arguments between traditionalists and progressivists — as though there could be a winner, or a refined balance between these positions, that has evaded everyone for the past century and a half. Nor can we look to any benefits from battles about whether the schools are there to produce "job-ready skills" (as a local school advertised its main product recently) as distinct from the fulfillment of each child's unique potentials.

I should perhaps add that educating people better doesn't require that we somehow solve the conflicts described above. For example, Zvi Lamm observes, "The relation between the individual, who possesses a sense of his own uniqueness, and society, which exerts pressure to level out individual differences and impose conformity, is complex and problematic" (1976, p. 127). I am not proposing to "solve" the problems inherent in this particular conflict between an individual's desire for freedom to develop his or her uniqueness and society's need for conformity. Rather, I am intent on describing a process of education in which this problem doesn't interfere. That is, I am suggesting that this problem, which has been one of the hindrances to schools' success for a century and a half, doesn't belong in a proper scheme of education. Such a claim may well seem likely to evade what everybody knows schooling is about — but you can guess my response to that, which will have something to do with Athenians and heifer livers. I'll sketch the outline of how we can reconceive education without such mutually conflicting ideas in the next chapter.

Of course, the "mission statements" of all schools, school districts, and state and federal educational institutions invariably, in my fairly exhausting surveys, promise all three of our incompatible goods. When we reach the plausible conclusion that these promises cannot be fulfilled, and that they constitute a form of nonsense, then we have to get back to the hard business of constructing an alternative that overcomes the problems and mutually conflicting beliefs of the currently dominant idea.

Education is a process in which something good is done to the mind. When we regret what has been done to someone's mind as a result of what they have learned we call it miseducation, indoctrination, or something less polite. Our problems about how to educate people have been tied up with our being unsure of what the mind is and, consequently, how to do the best for it. You will prescribe different things to improve the mind if you think of it primarily as an information-processing device rather than as the residence of the sinful soul or as an aesthetic organ. If someone's notion of the mind is wrong, there's not much hope for their prescriptions to improve it. Or, at least, the prescriptions will be inadequate in much the same way as the notion. The challenge for this chapter is to present a more adequate notion of the mind than has so far been common in the field of education, and to provide a set of prescriptions for properly educating such minds.

We know that the mind is connected with the brain somehow. The brain is a chunk of wrinkled stuff, and each of us has one that is uniquely our own, whereas the mind is made up of all kinds of things like language and culture, which we share in complicated ways with others — and which would exist even if you or I didn't. We have tried to make sense of our minds by means of analogies with our technology: clockworks and telephone systems had a misleading run, and now we are offered various analogies with computers. So we are invited to think of our brain as computer hardware and the mind as its operating system or the programs it is running.

One evident feature of our minds is that they are cultural organs. Humans have, for reasons that no doubt seemed evolutionarily good at the time, developed the means to store symbols outside our biological memory in such a way that we can access and retrieve their meaning at later times. It's been an immensely clever trick, but not without its costs, as we've seen already. Another common analogy — common, at least, since Vygotsky showed its utility — is to think of the relationship between this externally stored symbolic material and our brains as a bit like the relationship between tools and our bodies.

This analogy invites us to reflect on our peculiar use of tools. Many animals use tools for particular purposes — to winkle grubs out from decaying wood or to break shells, and so forth — but we seem to incorporate our tools in a quite distinctive manner. A new tool not only enables us to perform some specific task, it also changes our image of what we *can* do and even of what we are. Once we invent a tool for some purpose we become alert to what else we can do with it. Long ago, our first tools were not invented with the idea of building metal machines that fly or huge skyscrapers or space vehicles, but the accumulation of tools and imagined possibilities for their use has led to these constructions. Supplied with tools, our body becomes transformed in our minds in its potency and possibilities.

If we think of our accumulated store of external symbols as a kind of tool kit for the brain, we may use Vygotsky's analogy to explore how the brain becomes transformed by its incorporation of such tools. So literacy, for example, allowed us to leave records and retrieve them later, but after millennia of development, it has transformed our lives immeasurably. Once the tool of writing was invented for recording quantities of stored grain and wine, humans began to explore what other uses it could be put to. Although we began with simple utility, we have stretched our symbolic tools in the direction of unsuspected possibilities. The stretch may be like that in Flaubert's most famous lines from *Madame Bovary* about the uses of language: it "is like a honky-tonk on which we beat out tunes for bears to dance to, yet all the while we long to move the stars to pity." As the Hebrew God muttered, observing the human creatures trying to build a tower to the heavens: "Behold . . . how nothing will be restrained from them, from what they have imagined to do" (Genesis 11:6). Tools plus imagination make new worlds.

So this "external store of symbolic material" should be understood as the receptacle of our dreams as well as of our more utilitarian records. The building of this cultural storehouse is compared by Merlin Donald to a major evolutionary change in human intellectual functioning, and, he argues, we should see this cultural storehouse as having as much influence on the modern mind as the architecture of the brain itself (1991, 2001). That is, our brain and culture together create the lineaments of the mind. Our brains include many capacities, such as those for language and abstract thought, that are never realized in people who survive alone, apart from a culture; such brain capacities are not a part of the mind unless stimulated and developed within a culture.

If we see this external symbolic storehouse as something whose internalization in individuals' brains constructs their minds, and if we accept Vygotsky's idea that the tools, or "operating systems" and "programs," for our brains initially exist external to our bodies in our culture, then we may begin to conceive of education's tasks somewhat differently. Education becomes the process in which we maximize the tool kit we individually take from the external storehouse of culture. Cultural tools thus become cognitive tools for each of us.

Apart from its unfamiliar terms, this idea might not seem obviously different from current ideas about education. Everybody has seen education as a process in which we select from what is available in our culture that which will best enhance the brain's capacities. One trouble with this abstract and general discussion, of course, is that it may be too easy to shift words a little to hide differences or exaggerate them. Let me take this chapter, then, to work out in more detail how education would look different from current norms and practices if we saw it as a process of maximizing our cognitive tool kit.

What Are Cognitive Tools?

There is a short answer to this and a longer answer. The longer answer will take up most of this chapter, in which I will describe and give examples of the main cognitive tools that we should attend to in educating people. The short answer is that cognitive tools are the things that enable our brains to do cultural work. Our brains, like those of any animal, are responsible for controlling an array of physiological and social work. But we have also amassed that external symbolic material that constitutes our culture. As we learn features of our cultural inheritance, the brain is provided with the tools that enable it to realize various of its capacities. Alone, no one learns to speak, to read and write, or to think with theoretic abstractions. These potentials of human brains are actualized only by the brain learning, and learning to use, particular pieces from our cultural storehouse. Culture, as it were, programs the brain. It is simplistic to push the analogy of brain as computer and culture as operating systems and programs, but the analogy is helpful in so far as it locates a significant part of our minds in that cultural material.

I recall my very Catholic family being scandalized, but also guiltily amused, by a doctor who, on the mention of the word *soul*, said that he had cut up men and women, black and white, and he'd never found a soul in any of them. We might offer a related comment to those who believe that studies of the brain will expose the working of the mind. There is no mind in the brain until the brain interacts with the external symbolic store of culture. People who think we have souls don't expect them to be visible to the anatomist, and people who reflect on the mind shouldn't expect neurophysiologists to provide new knowledge that will alter our understanding of what we need to do to minds in order to educate them. Well, one can easily run into trouble pushing analogies too far. The point of this one is that the mind is nearly invisible in our current understanding of the brain, but it is very plainly visible when viewed in terms of the culture our brains interact with.

One trouble with giving the short answer to the question of what cognitive tools are is that it is so general that it doesn't make clear what differences for educating people follow from thinking of education as maximizing cognitive tools. It might help, in moving on to the longer answer, to consider some other features of our brain/computer analogy.

Perhaps you have at some point upgraded the operating system of your computer. The companies that make these complex software systems tell us — with balloons, flashing lights, and earnest managers of vast networks — that the upgrade will significantly increase our productivity, extend the speed, power, and reliability of the computer, and enable us to run even better programs than those we currently use, which the same company is generously willing to sell us. (I wrote this with a ballpoint pen: one of the less troublesome upgrades to the writing technology I favor).

But operating-system upgrades are rarely simple. Sometimes you discover that a neat little utility you have relied on in the past no longer runs under the new O.S., and there is no announcement about when there might be a new version. You find that some comfortable routines are disrupted, and you need to learn new work-arounds for unexpected problems. And odd things keep happening to your e-mail. And those files you had saved in . . . you no doubt recognize all this too painfully well. In general, though, you find that the new O.S. allows you to perform relatively easily functions that were previously cumbersome or impossible, and the programs that take advantage of the new O.S. enable you to work better and achieve some new tasks efficiently. That is, in general the new O.S. significantly improves what your computer hardware can do, but at a cost. Sometimes the cost is very small, sometimes quite big, and sometimes for some people in some circumstances the costs outweigh the benefits. We will find analogues to these costs and benefits in education.

If we think of our brains as analogous to our computer hardware, we may think of cognitive tools as having two forms, equivalent to operating systems and to programs. Below I will describe five somewhat distinctive "operating systems" that our culture makes available to our brains. These five major cognitive tool kits are available for downloading from our cultural storehouse. But their basic codes are complexly interrelated, so that for the optimum functioning of your mind they need to be downloaded in the sequence in which they were compiled in the first place. (O.S. 5, as it were, can't be successfully installed if you are running O.S. 2; you have to upgrade to O.S. 3 then O.S. 4 before you can get all the benefits of O.S. 5.)

Each O.S. enables you to run a large set of programs — smaller-scale cognitive tools. Many of the programs that ran under the previous O.S. will still run under the new system, some will not, and some will run but behave eccentrically. The task of education, given this analogy, is to ensure the fullest downloading from our culture of the five main "O.S." cognitive tool kits in proper sequence, and also to ensure the downloading of the maximum range of "programs," or cognitive tools, for each.

Again, this is a useful but limited analogy. The use will, I hope, become clear as I describe education in terms of maximizing our cognitive tool kits. The limit — or one limit — is that unlike computer operating systems the smaller-scale "programlike" cognitive tools are in part constituents of the "O.S." cognitive tools. But keep going, and I think you'll see what I mean.

The Mind's Operating Systems and Programs

The main cultural work that cognitive tools enable our brains to perform is understanding. Seeing education as a process of maximizing our cognitive tool kit, then, is to see it as a process of enlarging our understanding as far as possible given the tools our culture has developed. I will, therefore, describe the main "operating systems," or cognitive tool kits, as kinds of understanding, which I call somatic, mythic, romantic, philosophic, and ironic. (I have made some earlier attempts to describe these, summed up in Egan, 1997.) I will first give a general characterization of each kind of understanding and then describe a subset of "programs" — smaller-scale cognitive tools that work best with each "operating system" and are also — to break out of the analogy — constituents of the "operating system." At the end of the chapter I'll explore some additional features of this model of the mind and its implications for educating people.

Somatic Understanding

If we were to describe an animal — a vole, say, or an emu — we would focus on the distinctive features of its body and its array of senses and how these produce its typical behaviors within its normal environment. But when we set about describing ourselves — human beings, I mean (in case any future readers . . .) — we tend to forget we have bodies, except as containers for neurotransmitters, conscious-ness, language, and other brain-connected stuff. And, indeed, our brains are the most distinctive things about us — our giraffe's neck or peacock's tail. But we do have a distinctive body, and if we are going to make a general inventory of the tool kits available to us, it is with the body's tool kit that we should begin.

We should begin with the body because the array of its senses determines for us the basic meanings we can derive from our experi-ence of the world. Most basically, we perceive a certain range and scale of phenomena. Our dominant senses are vision, hearing, touch, taste, and smell, which we tend to value more or less in that order. Our language is accordingly full of metaphors built from those senses. You see what I mean?

These senses have so dominated our understanding that we have immense difficulty understanding the behavior of subatomic particles or models of the early conditions of the cosmos or other phenomena not readily gasped by our senses. As modern sciences have increas-ingly relied on mathematics to give accounts of conditions inaccessi-ble to our senses, the layperson has had to rely on interpreters who are gifted at finding approximating images that hint at what the math-ematics report. We can partially accompany Einstein when he de-scribes riding on a light-wave, but have to dismount when the visible cosmos turns into mathematical formulae. Christina Lamb describes the unlamented former Taliban education minister of Afghanistan scoffing at the credulity of Westerners who believe the sun is more than 90 million miles from the earth: "There is no tape measure long enough to reach it!" he reasonably pointed out (2003). Whatever we believe the distance is, it's an act of faith for most of us. Hard not to feel a little sympathy for someone who wants a way of measuring such distances based on familiar senses.

We have inherited an odd way of talking about our body, as though we think of "ourselves" as somehow apart from it. So we talk about body and soul, or mind and body. St. Francis of Assisi referred to his body as "Brother donkey." I'd be surprised if voles or emus categorized their sense of themselves like this. There are good and bad reasons why we have adopted this way of thinking about ourselves. The good reasons derive from the peculiar development of our brain, which has resulted in the languages and cultures that are so dominant in our lives. The bad reasons have to do with the inclination to forget somewhat that our brain is a part of our body and that our mind, despite incorporating cultural stuff we share in complex ways with others, is also fundamentally embodied. The particular kind of body we have determines our distinctive take on the world; the body's influence pervades even the most refined mental activity.

Our body shapes our language, from the physical structure of our pharynx, larynx, and tongue and the way these determine the array of sounds we can make, to the length of time it takes to ease our breath through these organs to chunk a set of language sounds into sentences — a case of syntax overriding carbon dioxide, in Steven Pinker's nice phrase (1994), though we might more appropriately see the limits of the sentence as carbon dioxide's triumphant determination of syntax — to the fundamental metaphors derived from bodily experience that provide "a pervasive principle of human understanding that underlies our vast network of interrelated literal meanings" (Johnson, 1987, p. 65). Johnson has shown how our bodily based concepts of "in," "out," "force," "balance," and so on, pervade our understanding of many of the world's processes. These basic concepts are publicly shared and understood by everyone, but each of us grasps them in slightly different ways as a result of our individual bodily experience and our emotional responses to that experience.

In a kind of despair about the consistent refusal to acknowledge the bodily sources of the meanings we construct from experience, Johnson notes, "The vast majority of books on linguistics and the philosophy of language assume that meaning is, first and foremost, something *sentences* have" (1987, p. 1; emphasis in original).

The brain's first job is to expand into the body, so to speak, to recognize patterns in the flailing around of outlying bits, like hands and fingers, and bring them into coordinated actions that serve the body's purposes. Babies engage early in reciprocal eye contact with others, they touch and are touched, they begin to copy voices which, reciprocally, copy theirs, and they begin a complex of imitations that set the ground rules for social interactions for the rest of their lives. These earliest bodily interactions "interlock the infant's growing mind with those of its caretakers and ultimately the broader society" (Donald, 2001, p. 255).

These foundational interactions are pervasively emotional. So a central feature of somatic understanding, and of our bodies' sense-making tool kit, is its emotional nature. These emotions persist and develop as the most basic orientors and organizers of our cognition throughout our lives. If I tell you that there has just been a revolution in an African or South American or North American country, your rational assessment of the event — Were the rebels led by a left-wing or a right-wing zealot? Did they have C.I.A. backing? Were they recently defeated in an election? Did neighboring dictators send support to the rebels or the government? — rides on top of emotions connected by association with those questions. Delight, distress, elation, horror, satisfaction, anger, compassion, and fear constitute elements of the underlying matrix that shapes your response to the revolution. David Kresch coined the neat term *perfinkers* to describe our cognition: we perceive, feel, and think together. If we recognize the foundational development of somatic understanding's emotional core, we will be less likely to see cognition, and cognitive tools, as somehow separate from our emotional lives; however sophisticated our thinking becomes it will always be oriented and shaped by the emotions of the body within which it occurs.

The early interlockings with others that begin with our bodily copying and responses — the peek-a-boo game, the mutual sticking out of tongues, the hiding and revealing, the weeping and the laughter — will later find their way into language. The rituals of expectation and satisfaction become stories; the pretend games become metaphors; our sense of humor becomes jokes; sequences and patterns become mathematics and rhymes, and so on. The exuberant language forms we develop between two and four years of age, and elaborate thereafter, all begin in the early bodily experience of infancy. That bodily foundation is not left behind in our later intellectual developments. (As a side note it seems, consequently, obvious to suggest that computers will never mimic human intelligence convincingly until they are integrated with, or can mimic integration with, our kind of body and its emotions.)

If the task at hand is to work out how best to educate people then we will have to attend in early childhood to the stimulation and development of the tool kit of somatic understanding, and to recognize that this tool kit does not cease to function as language develops but remains to be developed throughout life. The tools noted so far involve prominently our senses and the emotions involved in their use. Somatic education, then, will involve varied forms of stimulating babies' vision, using exposure to the natural world in as many of its forms as is possible, exposure to faces and their multiple expressions and to hands playing finger games, and similarly stimulation of their hearing, with rhythmic sounds and games, with language, and the array of squeaks and plops and clicks that humans can make — with a bit of practice. Most infants enormously enjoy games involving varied odd sounds associated with patterns of movement and touch. Well, I hardly need to elaborate on the kinds of games and loving care that parents commonly engage in and that engage all the senses. Somatic education, however, is the basis on which later education will build, and so extensive sensory stimulation, interaction, and play is important. Remember, too, that babies are like adults in most things, and will also value time to explore idly and to contemplate their lot.

Two prominent components of the somatic tool kit are humor and the emotions. Educators have typically neglected humor and emotions in their treatises, but their stimulation and development seem to me among the most important constituents of a program of education. The kind of games mentioned earlier can contribute toward the development of humor, but it is useful to remember that humor comes in many forms. The intentional interruption of any normal pattern of activity — even if that pattern has just been created for the game — can stimulate a humorous response. The interruption conditions the baby to incongruity. Incongruity is central to a wide array of forms of humor. Ability to deal easily and pleasurably with incongruity contributes to flexibility of mind. Flexibility of mind is an important component of an educated person. Humor is important for many things, not least the delight it can give to experience, but it has a distinctive educational importance in its contribution to flexible, imaginative, and creative thinking.

Somatic understanding, then, is maximized by stimulation and development of the senses, of humor, and of the emotions. Stimulation and development of these is the central activity before language develops that sets the foundation for an adequate educational program. While the importance of focusing primarily on the senses, humor, and the emotions will recede somewhat as language develops, they will nevertheless continue to be important components of educational development throughout life. The forms we should use for their continued stimulation and development will change and be significantly conditioned by the components of future kinds of understanding — as would be evident if you were to try playing peek-a-boo games with a fifteen- or forty-five-year-old on a bus. But throughout life, stimulating the senses, humor, and the emotions remains an important part of educating. (I recall reading that the late Canadian prime minister, Pierre Elliott Trudeau, each year took it upon himself to master some new physical skill. The account was accompanied by a picture of him, in his late fifties or early sixties, jumping from a sprung diving board. That year he had decided to learn how to do a somersault into the pool.)

We could add a number of further tools developed very early in life. Steven Mithen's *The Singing Neanderthals* (2005), for example, has helped to show how profoundly we are musical animals. Our musicality seems a central feature of our body's tool kit, perhaps, as Mithen suggests, from early in our evolution as modern humans. We walk according to particular patterns that easily lead us to dance, and we sing, and sing together, in ways that are profoundly central to being human. Our bodies seem to be unique in the animal world in the way we recognize, track, compose, and respond to patterns in the physical world (including patterns of sound) that seem to have no particular utility to us. This peculiarity of our sense making seems to give humans in all cultures, and perhaps babies more than anyone, great aesthetic delight.

Rhythm and pattern are recognized in some form by all animals, but humans' sense of both is rich and quickly bootstrapped into more complex forms that find expression through all our senses. We look for meaning in patterns from our earliest years, even when what we see, hear, or touch may be quite random. But we quickly recognize those recurring regularities that give us our most basic understanding of the world we find ourselves in, of its significant patterns of sound, sight, touch, taste, and smell. We begin to construct that uniquely human kind of meaning on the back of the patterned regularities our senses deliver to us.

Merlin Donald argues that "mimesis" — intentional representations that are invented — is central to early forms of humans' learning behavior (1991). While numerous other species mimic (or even, according to Donald's categorization, imitate) the physical movements and sounds of other individuals in their community, it is only humans that seem able to combine such gestures or sounds in novel ways, or indeed to invent new gestures derived from known ones. We use our bodies in interpreting the gestures of others, of course, as well as in inventing novel gestures for communicative purposes. Such types of interactions are further tools for achieving that process Donald describes: interlocking the infant's growing mind with those of its caretakers and ultimately the broader society.

If you are sitting next to a one-year-old and a cat and you point at the door, the toddler will usually look at the door and the cat will look at your finger. The toddler will also point to things, something the cat, or a chimpanzee, will not do. We very early develop the power to read the intentions of others in their actions and anticipate their reading ours in our actions. We represent the world in the mind, and relate to the external world so composed in the mind, in a way that is unique among our fellow animals.

For sure, this is barely scraping the surface of what constitutes ideal somatic understanding, and the few components of this kind of understanding have been sketched only summarily. But my aim here is just to try to establish a new way of conceiving education, in terms of maximizing cognitive tools, and while proper development of somatic understanding in infancy is important for all that is to follow, the distinctiveness of this approach will become clearer when dealing with the kinds of understanding that usually occupy school years.

Mythic Understanding

The seemingly miraculous development of language affects each child like a new operating system for the brain. Language programs the brain to take on new tasks, to change and enhance some old ones, and to diminish others. I'm calling this kind of understanding "mythic" because it has significant features in common with the kind of thinking found in oral cultures throughout the world and in our own culture's prehistory. All societies with sophisticated language but no writing system have certain kinds of stories, which have been called "myths" because they seemed very like the myth stories of ancient Greece.

(Making a comparison between modern children's understanding and that of adults in oral cultures is dangerous, of course. Such comparisons were made in the past to justify colonialism and racist policies. In part, the comparisons led to such conclusions because of the false theories of social progress and individual development people held at the time. Along with the general recognition of how improper and disastrous such comparisons were has come a kind of horror of even contemplating any such comparisons at all. This increasingly seems an outworn overreaction. If we think about human thinking in terms of the cognitive tools available, and we find that young children and members of oral cultures share the use of language without literacy, we will discover many common influences on their cognition, and the study of one can assist the understanding of the other. Dangers arise only when we try to draw inappropriate conclusions and make unsupported generalizations or suggest that their uses of the available cognitive tools are the same — which they patently are not.) It has been common to refer to young children, and to oral cultures, as "preliterate" — as though becoming literate is a natural development for human beings. It is easy to forget that literacy is a recently invented trick, whose enormous utility has made nearly everyone want to learn and exploit it. But in endlessly varied cultures through indeterminate generations our species has had a wholly human experience of the world without literacy. So I want to describe mythic understanding as composed of a rich array of cognitive tools that are not "pre" something else that will come to complete it; it is complete in itself as a distinctive way of making sense of the world. Literacy will come later like a new operating system for most modern children, but we can best prepare them to learn and exploit literacy if we first focus on helping them to learn and exploit the resources of their oral language.

So what do these constituents of oral language that program our brains look like and how do they generate a distinctive kind of understanding? Well, here's a brief and mixed list of some constituents to start with: stories, metaphors, binary structuring and mediating, rhyme and rhythm, pattern, jokes, forming images from words, play, puzzles, and the recognition of mystery. No doubt one could add to this list, or make it a more coherent set, but it should be enough to allow me to show how these cognitive tools contribute to a distinctive kind of understanding and why they should be the focus of educating children between the time language becomes fluent and before literacy becomes fluent.

What kind of "tool" is the story? It's the kind of tool that enables you to understand how to feel about events. Stories shape experience and knowledge into forms that uniquely can establish their emotional meaning. That is, stories don't simply convey information and describe events, they shape their contents so that we will feel good or bad, joyful or sorrowful, as we hear about them. No other form of language can do this. If I were to tell you about a generous and skilled doctor and add, "It was a hot day and the doctor dived into the water," you may feel a small pleasure for her. But when I further tell you "the water was crowded with hungry sharks," you may feel some regret or distress. The story could continue with the information that she was trying out a new shark repellant, or that she was risking her life to save a child who had fallen into the water. Your feelings about her diving into the water would change depending on the subsequent events. You would know you have reached the end of the story when you know how to feel about her diving in and the other events — in this case our feelings will also be significantly shaped by whether the doctor later had or was lunch.

The trouble with our lives, as you may have noticed, is that they don't have any clear meaning, except in as far as we can fit them into stories. That is, some people create or inherit very crude stories that provide them with security and freedom from anxiety but not much understanding of human experience's potential richness. The young Nazi indoctrinated into party beliefs would not usually face the kind of angst and insecurities of those who refuse to adopt so crude a story to make sense of their experience. Life, it can seem, is just one damn thing after another. For daily meaning, we plot our current activities into some general story to enable us to orient ourselves, to choose priorities, to know how to feel.

Fed up with this argument — which seems to deny any meaning to your life except what you construct for yourself from a story or accept from some authoritative source's story — you hurl this book across the room, glad to be rid of it, and instead pick up the *National Inquirer* or *Finnegans Wake*. The book, however, hits the side of the mantel, ricochets to the left, and knocks to the floor that unusual and large green vase your mother-in-law brought last week. Now do you feel glad or sorry you threw the book away? You clean up the pieces of the vase and see among the shards a lottery ticket you bought yesterday and couldn't find. You scratch the gray areas of the ticket and discover that you have won $1,000 per week for life! Now are you glad or sorry that you threw the book? You celebrate by buying that neat European sports car you have long wanted, and driving it back from the show-room you and the car get scrunched by an out-of-control SUV. You die. Now are you glad or sorry that you threw the book? My point is not that something bad is likely to happen to people who throw this book around, but rather that we determine the emotional meaning of the events of our lives by building them into provisional stories. But our real-life stories, and the stories we use to shape history, remain provisional. As new things happen we have to be ready to re-allot significance and meaning and re-assess our emotional evaluation and responses to events. The delight of fictional stories is that they end, and so we can fix the emotional meaning of the events from which they are composed. Life and history, when reflected on with any sophistication, deny us the security of fixed meaning.

So stories not only deal with fictional material but can also be used to shape factual material. When your boss asks "What's the story on the new account?" she isn't asking you to make up a fiction. She is asking you to describe the new account and its circumstances in a clear way that brings out what is important about it, and that consequently tells the boss how to feel about it. Similarly, the newspaper editor's asking "What's the story on the stadium riot?" isn't inviting a fiction but rather wants an account shaping the events into an emotionally clear form. It is this power of the story form to shape emotional responses to its contents that makes it of such educational importance during these early years. We want to tell children what the great stories are about the world in which we find ourselves: about our mathematics, about human societies and history, about our sciences, and so on. While there is an important place for fictional stories in young children's education, there is also a perhaps more pervasive role for using elements of the story form in order to shape knowledge of the factual world into emotionally and imaginatively engaging lessons and units of study. The story form can help us to bring out clearly for children the wonder of the real world and help them to see and feel that wonder.

The trick to doing this routinely will turn on our using a little ingenuity in analyzing just what are the features of stories that enable them to have their powerfully engaging effects, and then working out how we can apply these to algebra, punctuation, and all the other stuff of an educational curriculum. I'll show how we can do this fairly easily later in the book. But there are other cognitive tools that can shape lessons, make knowledge imaginatively engaging to young children, and enlarge their mythic understanding.

There are a thousand books about the educational, social, emotional, psychological, and so forth, importance of telling fictional stories to young children, so I won't add much to them here. But it might be worth pointing out that if using the story form is an important tool for the adequate development of the mind, making children familiar with a wide array of stories is clearly important. Understanding varied ways in which stories work adds to the flexibility of the mind. Learning to follow stories, and to construct one's own, is a foundation of education. The story is our best tool for helping one person understand what it is like to be someone else. We can thereby enlarge our understanding of others and enlarge our sympathy. The storehouse of modern and traditional stories from a wide variety of cultures is an important resource for a whole range of educational purposes.

Of course stories have been, and are, used to indoctrinate children. The indoctrination works if the stories all have a common message — about the superiority of one's social group and the wickedness or stupidity of all others. The best defense against this kind of indoctrinating is not crudely to censor stories, but rather to ensure that children are introduced to a great variety of them.

The kinds of stories that most commonly engage young children's attention use another prominent cognitive tool. Think of the Grimm fairy stories and their almost universal appeal to children, West and East and in between. Each story, just below its surface, has a simple structural element. Emotionally charged binary opposites — like courage/cowardice, security/fear, love/hate, good/bad — provide the main element that gives shape and provides access to the meaning of the events. The story of Hansel and Gretel would be just one thing after another if it weren't carefully structured to attach our emotions of security and fear to the sequence of events. The story plays with those emotions and their interactions and conflicts. How fearful that the children should be hungry and lost in the forest; what a relief that they find an edible cottage and are invited in; how fearful that the wicked witch . . . Again, the educational trick will involve abstracting this feature of binary structures from fairy stories and seeing how it can be used in teaching algebra, history, or whatever.

A part of the folklore of educators at present, which has always bewildered me, is that young children are "concrete" thinkers. Now clearly this idea captures something about the way young children's thinking differs from adults'; but it is generally taken to mean that young children therefore can't understand abstractions, among other intellectual deficiencies they are presumed to labor under. The trouble with such folklorish beliefs is that they then prevent those who hold them from seeing children except through those beliefs. But consider the foundations of those Grimm fairy stories — security/fear, courage/cowardice, good/bad: what more abstract ideas have you ever learned? Think also of the characters — they are not people in any rounded sense but representatives of beauty, simplicity, greed, terror, goodness, and so on. That is, it's not just the underlying structure of the story that rides on abstractions but the characters also embody abstractions.

Young children do not usually use *theoretic* abstractions, but their thinking is constantly suffused with abstractions. Indeed it seems to make better sense than to claim that young children are concrete thinkers to claim that they make sense of the "concrete" better when it is tied to underlying abstractions. It is the abstractions — love, hate, fear, security, anxiety, good, bad — that are more profoundly known and pervasively used in their thinking. Our educational program, then, will be sure to draw on, to stimulate, and to elaborate children's use of abstractions. These emotionally charged abstractions are clearly another cognitive tool we will sensibly try to develop: another utility of our new oral language operating system.

The Grimm fairy tales, and children's games, and most of what engages young children's imaginations are built on these abstract, emotionally charged binary opposites. And if early schooling is to introduce children to the great stories and games of our culture — our history, science, mathematics, literature, and so on — we would surely be a little dense to ignore the structural feature we can see in all those other areas of their spontaneous engagement. Again, it might take a little ingenuity to see how to present mathematics and history in such terms, while ensuring they do not falsify what we want to teach. But only a little ingenuity is required, and the rewards in terms of children's understanding can be enormous.

As time and experience, and education, continue, children learn to mediate between the opposites that provide their first grappling tools on knowledge. We each learn to build a conceptual world between the extremes — between the ideally good and the bad, the totally secure and the dangerous, the infinitely courageous and the cowardly. Education is a process of elaborating that conceptual middle world to more adequately reflect in language the world we experience. But our adult recognition that the binary terms we begin with are not adequate representations of the complex reality should not lead us either to fail to recognize or deny their utility in the earliest attempts to grapple with areas of knowledge.

When a vole scurries around on a windy day, it is unlikely that it sees the waving grasses as being like the turmoil in its soul about its relationship with a prospective mate. But a part of the great tool kit we acquire with language — a component of our new operating system — is precisely this odd ability to see one thing in terms of another that may be entirely unconnected with it. Humans frequently see weather or natural objects as representing their emotions; indeed, almost anything can be seen in terms of anything else.

This enormously fertile capacity for metaphor seems to develop as a fundamental utility for our symbolizing. If the arbitrary sounds we can make are to be understood as stable meanings by others we must, most basically, be able to see the symbols of speech in terms of the things we use them to refer to. Obvious, but it's really weird. We have learned to shape the air coming out of our lungs to make a fairly large array of sounds and then agree that various of these sounds will mean certain things. Metaphor thus suffuses language. Every sentence is made up from metaphors we have, usually, forgotten were metaphors.

Being able to see these often-invisible or forgotten metaphors is one tool of creative language use — it allows us to play with what otherwise we are constrained by. Metaphor enables us more richly to express what we mean and, reciprocally, to understand complex messages from others that enrich what we can mean.

In educating, then, and — to use our two casual metaphors — equipping children with the cognitive tools in the great tool kit of language, or deploying all the utilities of our new operating system, we will want to focus on stimulating and developing children's ability to recognize and use varied, rich metaphors. The flexibility and creativity of their thinking is clearly tied up with this skill, so we would be unwise to ignore it or leave it to chance in our program of education. One of the costs of failing to develop our metaphoric capacity is the kind of literal thinking that never gets beyond its starting assumptions and presuppositions. It is thinking that is closer to calculating than to anything critical or imaginative: thinking not only condemned to remain in "the box" but not even knowing there is an outside to one's box. Well, we're all boxed to a greater or lesser degree, of course, but one role of education is at least to expand the box and make clear that it does have an outside that may be worth the struggle to occasionally visit.

Another related and even more peculiar tool that comes along with language is our ability to form mental images from the words we hear. Indeed, we seem unable not to exercise this further peculiar tool that is associated with a large cubic-centimeterage of our brains devoted to symbolizing. Consider: Signor Bartoli gained weight after retiring from the lace-making business. He moved to a villa that overlooked Lake Geneva. Today, as every morning, he sits in a cane chair on the balcony outside his bedroom, reading the London *Independent* newspaper, while he drinks black coffee and nibbles toast generously spread with marmalade. The large plate on his breakfast tray is smeared with the remains of the two over-easy eggs he has consumed along with large helpings of bacon and mushrooms. He adjusts his dressing gown, noticing through the leafless poplars that the rising mist, a violet film, pale and more translucent than the most diaphanous gauze, is gradually exposing the gray waters of the lake.

You have probably more or less involuntarily generated a picture in your mind that has been, oddly, stimulated by the above few lines of inky squiggles on paper. Each reader of this will have formed a somewhat different image. We refer to them as "images," as though they are internal versions of external pictures, but, of course, they are not. In some of your images the smell of coffee will have occurred; some of you may have supplied Signor Bartoli with a glass-topped table, though nothing is mentioned as holding up his breakfast tray. And, even odder, you may have felt some small, fleeting dislike for dear old Bartoli, while some may have generated a tiny note of sympathy to color their image.

This peculiar act, in which I have encouraged you shamelessly to engage, is clearly tied up with what we call imagination. Generating images from words is one of the powerful cognitive tools that come along with oral language. Its immense utility was discovered long ago in the creation of shared images and feelings about who "we" — our family, tribe, or nation — are, what we are doing here, and what we are supposed to do for the time we are here. In tandem with the story, this tool provides the conceptual glue that binds people together in society and generates their sense of solidarity and identity. Americans learn a story about their country's founding and identity, and they learn a set of images, with appropriate emotional responses that support the story. Oddly enough, other countries do the same, in their peculiarly different ways — their stories and their potent images leave "us" cold.

Given the range of social and psychological functions this image-forming tool allows us to perform, it is clearly something we need to use in educating and a tool we need, in turn, to educate. That is, when teaching mathematics, science, or history we need to attend beyond the concepts and knowledge to the images that can make the concepts and knowledge engaging and vivid. We will also be sensible to consider the conditions, apart from frequent use, that will stimulate increasing flexibility and sophistication in use of this tool. You may scan educational textbooks till your brain crumbles, but you will find hardly any notice of image generation from words, and no discussion of how teachers can stimulate and develop it.

Most commonly today we don't simply ignore this cognitive tool but we almost seem intent on suppressing it. The young child today is bombarded with images. TV, of course, is the great enemy of this tool's development, constantly providing images and undermining exercise of the capacity to generate one's own images from words. We encourage instead the easy generation of stereotypical images. We, similarly, give children storybooks full of illustrations. Nearly all young children will be engaged more by an oral story told by an adult—even when told hesitantly, stumblingly—than by one read with many visually attractive illustrations. At least, this is the case when children have actually heard a story told. Many children today never experience this. Either they watch movies, or TV, or, at best, have a story read to them while they look at the pictures. Given the importance of generating images from words in the development of the imagination, many children—often those from affluent backgrounds—suffer impoverishment of this tool from the beginning. So we will want to do something about this in our educational program.

Now consider these items. A boy fell into the sea and thrashed around shouting: "I can't swim! I can't swim!" A girl stood looking at him from the shore: "So what? I can't play the violin, but I don't go shouting about it." Perhaps you heard about the weightlifter who was visiting town for the games and looking for a room to rent. The landlady said, "It's six hundred dollars for the week." The weightlifter said, "How much is it for the strong?" Maybe you've heard about the lion that became a cannibal and had to swallow his pride? My uncle has a dog with no legs. I asked, "What do you call him?" He said, "It doesn't matter. He won't come." Did you hear about the prisoner who spoke so slowly that it took him ten years to finish a sentence?

Yes, I know—you groaned inwardly rather than laughed. That's because you aren't six years old (I recklessly assume). The purpose of that paragraph was to point out something else that is blindingly obvious—that young children enjoy a certain kind of joke, and that humor is an important part of their lives, unless suppressed by adults for one sick reason or another. The obviousness of this observation seems indeed to have blinded educators—at least, as evidenced by shelf loads of educational textbooks that never mention it—to the fact that humor is a cognitive tool that comes along with language, and it is a tool that enables us to enlarge our understanding and pleasure in life. These are worthy educational goals, and so humor will be a consistent part of the educational program we are working towards. Somatic humorous games and sounds now find a vastly enriched arena for their exercise and development in language.

All the jokes in the earlier paragraph, even the dog joke, play with language in such a way that to get the joke, you have to recognize the language game being played. You have to see language as an object on which you can reflect. Language is as much a human behavior as the working of your liver, but it is one of these odd shared behaviors that make culture possible. Becoming conscious of it, and being able to reflect on it, are prerequisites to developing increasingly flexible language use, and that is prerequisite to a huge range of cultural attainments.

It is a pity perhaps that I feel it prudent first to indicate a serious utilitarian purpose for development of the sense of humor and only second to justify it in terms of its intrinsic value. The person whose sense of humor is developed well in early years and is stimulated throughout the educational program, should reap best the fruits of irony, which is a central characteristic of the educated person in this scheme. It is one of those things that enhances and enlarges our understanding in endless subtle and important ways.

It would be possible to describe a further series of cognitive tools that come along with language, but the above may be sufficient to indicate how looking at the possibilities of the great tool kit of language can lead us to a somewhat unusual way of approaching education. Let me mention briefly one further tool, which will further indicate the difference for educating that will follow from adopting this approach.

Do you know what state in the U.S. is named for Julius Caesar? Would you like to know? I'll give you a clue. In 56 B.C.E. Caesar invaded Britain, and after a summer of campaigning he withdrew his army to some islands off the coast of Gaul. They became known as Caesar's Islands, *Insulae Caesareae*. Over the centuries *Caesareae* degenerated into *Jersey*. So New Jersey is actually New Caesar. What is it about such puzzles that engages our interest? And why, if you didn't already know the answer, will you remember it forever? And if we can answer those questions, wouldn't we be silly to fail to use puzzles in educating children?

Voles and emus do not give any suggestion that the world for them is a place of mystery and wonder. The recognition of mystery is another cognitive tool associated with language. A strange task we have engaged with since we developed oral language involves our struggle to find ways of capturing and expressing in symbols whatever we discover about the world and experience. Our store of knowledge is pitifully small — however fast it may seem to be accumulating. One problem with much early schooling at the moment is that the world is presented to children as a kind of vast encyclopedia, of which they are learning the first elementary bits. In the classroom, the child is situated as a novice being gradually inducted into our vast realm of knowledge. And, of course, this in part captures what early schooling is about. But science, for example, is represented as a relatively prosaic accumulation of facts contained in textbooks, and the set of textbooks line up one after the other through to the final years of schooling, and then even bigger ones grind on through college years. The world, in short, is presented to the child as known, and, for the most part, as rather dull: interior opposite angles are congruent, and a thousand other such theorems, without much sense of their human meaning or importance, can weigh down the spirit during the early years of schooling. Where the wonders of math and science should live energetically and fruitfully in students' minds there are, for nearly all students today, vast and empty deserts.

Isaac Newton in his later years was praised by his nephew for the numerous and wonderful scientific and mathematical achievements that had won him great fame; he replied that he should rather be seen as being like a boy on a seashore diverted by a smoother pebble or a prettier shell than ordinary, while before him the great ocean of knowledge lay unnoticed. This image suggests that what we know is tiny and inconsequential compared to what is to be known. Not foolishly, we congratulate ourselves as a species for bringing more and more knowledge into the bright circle of our recognition. But we too rarely attend to how vast and mysterious is the unknown that extends perhaps infinitely beyond that small circle. We are surrounded by mysteries — not in some New Age-ish or sentimental or even spiritual sense. But all that we know is so fragmentary and insecure that an important part of education is to introduce children to the mystery that surrounds our knowledge even as we introduce them to the knowledge. The knowledge we teach needs to be seen against the huge backdrop of the unknown and perhaps unknowable. J. B. S. Haldane said that the universe is not just queerer then we imagined but is queerer than we can imagine. Behind and beyond the known is a sense of mystery that is crucial to the educated mind, and before which it is good to develop the attitude expressed in W. B. Yeats's "Everything we look upon is blest!" Blest in the sense of wonderful, strange, and knowable in only limited ways. The point of this long meandering paragraph is not to suggest we induce stupor in children's minds about how pathetically little they can learn, and so encourage them not to bother, but rather to show them how precious and how wonderful is the knowledge that we have, with mysterious ingenuity, carved out of the unknown. What a strange adventure! — that is the attitude that needs to be taught to children who are embarking on it.

Romantic Understanding

The next major upgrade of the brain's operating system, in history and in our education, is brought about by the acquisition of literacy, or, at least, by the way literacy has come to be used in our cultural history. Walter Ong describes it in slightly different terms: "Writing is a technology that transforms thought" (1982, p. x). Along with literacy come cognitive tools that can profoundly transform our minds' power and its capacity for understanding. Here is a brief list of some of the cognitive tools tied to the development of literacy: a new sense of reality, focus on the extremes of reality, association with heroic qualities, a sense of wonder, hobbies and collections, narrative understanding, recognizing knowledge through its human meaning, revolt, and idealism. One might add many others. Let's explore some of them in more detail and see why thinking about education in these kinds of terms might enable us to do the job better.

It is worth emphasizing at the beginning, perhaps inconveniently, that one can learn to read and write without any of the cognitive tools of "romantic understanding" becoming prominent in one's thinking. That is, literacy can refer to simple reading and writing for basic utilitarian purposes that have only minimal influence on the brain's functioning. It's a little like buying a powerful new system upgrade for your computer and continuing to use only your old word processor and e-mail program, neither of which takes advantage of the potential of the system upgrade. Or, in terms of the other metaphor I used earlier, literacy may give us access to the great treasure-house of culture, but by itself it doesn't open the further doors through which we can exploit and enjoy its riches. For that we need to develop the cognitive tools that come along with literacy.

So literacy is a brain upgrade with remarkable potential for enhancing the mind's functioning, but it can also be used for quite trivial purposes. Look at the material around your grocery store checkout and you'll see what I mean. This isn't intellectual snobbery; it's about educating people and getting the greatest pleasure and utility out of one's intellect. Checkout reading is to the mind what fatty and salty fast food is to the body. A person may prefer fast food, but it is not the choice to make if one wishes to get the greatest pleasure and utility out of one's body. An educational program will have to concern itself with how literacy can be developed for maximum benefit to the individual.

The first cognitive tool listed above in the tool kit of literacy is a new sense of reality. But clearly before they become literate most children distinguish between their fantasy worlds and reality. What is new about the postliterate sense of reality? Well, perhaps we can see it most clearly in the kinds of stories children enjoy pre-and postliteracy. At age four or five, magic is acceptable if it carries the plot forward; witches, dragons, and talking middle-class bears and rabbits in peculiar nonplaces and nontimes are staples of early childhood literature. The characters of such stories, as we saw above, are not "human" (even when animals) so much as embodiments of single qualities such as goodness, wickedness, greed, kindness, and so forth. At age nine or ten, children may still enjoy fantasy stories, but they have to be given a rational, even if utterly implausible, explanation for the fantasy features — such as Superman's powers or the Hulk's strength. Giants who manage to live on the top of clouds, or fairy godmothers, are not put to the same reality tests as the ten-year-olds' superheroes. Relatedly, the characters in postliterate stories, however simple they may be, have become recognizably human. Think of the difference between the rabbit characters and behavior of Beatrix Potter's Peter Rabbit and Hazel and Bigwig in Richard Adams's *Watership Down*.

This is just one small index of a fundamental shift in the way literate minds are inclined to make different sense of the world and of their experience. More generally, literacy led, in our cultural history, to a sense of an "objective" reality, which exists according to its own rules and laws that are quite independent from and immune to our hopes, fears, and wishes. It can lead each of us to this same recognition. One way we can secure this insight is to learn a lot about reality, using the disciplines of inquiry that were developed as a further product of literacy.

With the recognition of this new sense of reality, the mind is inclined to focus on reality's extent, its limits, and its most salient features. So, too, students who are becoming increasingly fluent in reading and writing and are beginning to learn about the world around them seek information about how extensive reality is, what are its limits, and what is most dramatic and wonderful about it. One of the stranger bits of dogma to have infected teacher education programs is that students are best or only able to deal with their immediate environments and experience, and so any attempt to teach them about more distant knowledge must always start with what they are familiar with. But ten- and eleven-year-old girls I know are most interested in spies, vampire slayers, and seriously weird pop stars, and the boys are into superheroes, supernaturally inarticulate sports stars, and creatures from outer space. Both really want to know who had the longest fingernails ever, what is the longest worm, and how many species of insects there are, give or take the odd billion, for every human being on the planet. Extreme sizes of body parts are also a big interest generator.

If you want to discover the extent and wonders of reality, it is a bizarrely inappropriate strategy to keep focusing on the here and now everyday life of students. Yet this has become one of the dogmas taught to every pre-service teacher in the Western world. As a direct consequence, typical students find algebra and social studies and most of what they do in school, and school itself, commonly boring. Now, I shouldn't overdo this, as is too easy. Many teachers do indeed make algebra exciting to students, or rather they bring out what is truly exciting about algebra so that students can experience it. And many students find school really interesting, even despite — they commonly add — what they are supposed to do in classes.

So if we want to work out how to educate people, we will be interested in how best to develop the set of cognitive tools that come along with literacy, and — for this first tool — we will want to make sure that students develop a vivid sense of the reality they find themselves in. This will involve learning a lot about reality — about history, cosmology, physics, mathematics, literature, and so on. But the initial aspects of history, cosmology, and so on, that we will focus on are what I'm calling the "romantic" parts. Romance might be defined as the desire to transcend the boundaries of reality while recognizing that one is constrained by those boundaries. It has within it a kind of ambivalence, neatly expressed in the figure of the typical romantic hero — whether Galahad or Superman or Anne of Green Gables. They all seek to overcome the limits and constraints that hem them in; they are heroic in that they do overcome some limits even while they recognize there are limits they cannot overcome. Only kryptonite has held me back!

Does this principle — that is, approach teaching about the real world through its most extreme, exotic, and wonderful features — threaten to confuse education with entertainment? Well, I suppose it's the more glitzy, superficial, sensational, trivial-spectacle, learning-empty sense of entertainment that is meant in the objection. But I'm not sure we will want to dismiss even some of these features of entertainment. The "romantic" attitude is one in which *everything* is in some way wonderful—"everything we look upon" again. So our study of earthworms may begin with the longest species, the fattest, the smallest, the longest lived, the quantity of in a square kilometer, the species that tills the most soil, the greatest distance ever traveled, the most colorful, the most exotic mating styles, and so on. Approaching a unit on the earthworm in sensationalist fashion, with the triviality of interest of a *Guinness World Records* entry, engages the "romantic" mind. The not hugely difficult task for the teacher then is to show that *everything* about earthworms is wonderful, fascinating, and sensational. This isn't so difficult, because it is true. The problem for the teacher is to understand what engages the imagination of the newly literate mind and present knowledge in a form that is readily accessible. This isn't pandering to appetites for sensationalism; it's a simple matter of common sense and courtesy.

Even if it is true that students' fascination with reality comes alive particularly when they learn about its extremes and limits, and its exotic or wonderful features, some educators clearly think this is regrettable and should be ignored or suppressed. But if we pause and consider what is the best strategy for learning about this vast reality you find yourself in, the "romantic" approach makes a good deal of sense. One problem with focusing on the local environment is that the student has no proportionate sense of it. Only when one has some sense of its scale and diversity can one feel confident in assessing the meaning of one's local environment and experience. So the long-used principle of "making lessons relevant to the student's experience" has usually had the opposite effect from that intended. Lacking a sense of context, the "relevant" remains frustratingly unfocused and drained of meaning. Paradoxically, it is by focusing on the limits and extremes of reality that one builds the context within which the "relevant" can become meaningful. This is, after all, the kind of strategy you would use if you found yourself in a strange environment. You would explore the limits of the town, its main features, where the river goes through it, where the central square is, what are the rituals and ceremonies of the natives, what kind of unusual clothes they wear, and so on.

What else happens with the literacy upgrade? What other cognitive tools develop to enable students' imaginations to grasp reality? Well, try to recall what it was like when you were eleven and trying to deal with the small or great anxieties created by trying to make sense of, and fit into, a real world that was not always hospitable. (A. E. Housman's line: "I, a stranger and afraid / In a world I never made," resonates very powerfully in early adolescence.) One strategy nearly all students use is to "romantically" associate with whomever or whatever seems best able to overcome the threats that hem them in. That is, they associate with heroes. Heroes are the people, or institutions, or whatever, that adolescents see as able to overcome the constraints that they feel hemmed in by. So the sports star or pop singer or historical character or family member can become a hero to a boy or girl. Having a hero is not a passive condition. The student—or you and I—vicariously partake in the hero's transgression of the boundaries that we cannot or do not cross. The sports or pop stars don't worry that they don't have enough money for the latest portable music player, or that they don't have enough cash to take the bus home, or that they have to wear what their mother tells them to wear; they don't seem to feel as though they are "strangers and afraid" because they have the power the students, and you and I, lack to remake our reality closer to our heart's desire.

And the educational point? Mathematics, science, history, and literature are crammed with heroes, so thickly there's barely room to stand up. The student lacks the ingenuity to work out what earthly use is the knowledge that alternate interior angles are congruent. Let me introduce you to the heroic Eratosthenes of Alexandria. They wouldn't know how to build railroads across rivers, under rivers, through miles of rock. Let me introduce you to Isambard Kingdom Brunel. The "romantic" perspective on reality is thronged with people, or rather with people who embody human emotions and extreme and exotic and wonderful characteristics—like courage, loyalty, compassion, ingenuity, envy, treachery, greed, and so on. The students don't so much associate with the hero, with the pop or the sports star; they associate with the transcendent human qualities the heroes embody. So the educational trick is to show the mathematics or the science or whatever as a product of some person's "transcendent human qualities" — that is, someone's extraordinary ingenuity, courage, treachery, compassion, and so on.

Everything in the curriculum can be shown in such a light. At present, mathematics and science texts, especially, are human deserts. You would never guess that all that knowledge was a product of people's passions, courage, deviousness, hopes, and fears. If we want that knowledge to engage the imaginations of early adolescents we need to show it in terms of people's passions, courage, and so on. It isn't very difficult to do this. Indeed, it is more enjoyable and meaningful for teachers and students alike, but we have created a system in which the importance of human emotions for meaning seems barely noticed. The result is commonly sterility in the knowledge presented, and boredom in those to whom it is presented and, often enough, in the teachers who are doing the presenting. It need not be so.

The sense of mystery and puzzles in the preliterate period become transmuted by literacy and its concern with reality into a sense of wonder. This sense of wonder can be stimulated and developed into a key tool of inquiry. All science, all inquiry, begins with the feeling we put into words as "I wonder . . ." During the half dozen or so years during which the cognitive tools of literacy are gaining an increasing hold over the brain's functioning and are enhancing the mind, the sense of wonder constantly serves to keep the world and experience interesting. It is the great enemy of taking things for granted. In the classroom it can be used to bring out what is wonderful by focusing students' attention on unexpected dimensions of reality and the human qualities connected with *anything*.

Consider the paper you are looking at, and which is messed up by the inky squiggles that constitute these words. (And if you are looking at the Klingon version on a screen . . . well, imagine.) Feel how smooth the paper is, of an astonishing uniform white, how thin the page is, and how easily you can turn one sheet over to read what is on its back. What astonishing ingenuity has gone into creating such an object — the scores of sheets stacked so precisely together. The more you know about the history of paper making, and of the people who made the various inventions that have culminated in this wonderful product, the easier it is to make that wonder vivid for students — and the more they learn about the chemical and physical inventions and processes, and of the people who made them, the longer that wonder will last, be passed on to others, and daily add in perhaps a small way to their delight every time they see a book. It is a technique for making our lives more rich and abundant with endless small delights.

A side note, repeating a point made earlier related to the previous components of our literacy upgrade: The cleverness of writing seduces us into taking it for granted and seeing it as something other than it is. We have become so clever at converting some aspects of our knowledge into these odd squiggles that we confusedly assume the squiggles contain knowledge. We can say, "the library is full of knowledge" without feeling stupid, even though it is entirely false, or rather, a subtle metaphor. There is no knowledge in the library, nor on a computer's hard drive, as I pointed out in the previous chapter. There are codes of various kinds, which, with ingenuity, we can reconstitute as knowledge. Knowledge exists only in living tissue in our bodies; what exists in libraries and computers are codes. People are the only repositories of knowledge. Forgetting the metaphorical sense in which we casually refer to books or computers containing knowledge is usually no problem. But forgetting that it is a metaphor, and taking it literally, has had a catastrophic effect on education. The problem has grown around the false notion that the codes are the ideal form of knowledge, and so teachers try to make students' minds mimic our coding system. So there has developed in education a notion of learning that implies that students' minds should store information, without recognizing that the brain just isn't very good at reliably storing coded information in the manner of a textbook or an encyclopedia. But human brains can amass huge amounts of knowledge if it is put into forms that human brains are good at learning. The book and computer accept any codes in any sequence. The human mind is good at learning when knowledge is made meaningful and emotionally charged and imaginatively engaging. It isn't hard to work out how to make knowledge fit those criteria, which take a somewhat different character at the different stages of education. At the stage following the onset of efficient literacy and preceding the onset of efficient theoretic thinking, the kinds of considerations I have touched on above indicate how we can go about making knowledge meaningful, emotionally charged, and imaginatively engaging. What we have in books are inert codes; the trick of transmuting those codes back into knowledge in new minds is to show it in the context of human hopes, fears, and passions.

Again, it would be easy to rattle on at even greater length identifying further cognitive tools of literacy, but let the above set of characteristics suffice to indicate how thinking about education in these terms leads to rather different principles from those that dominate schooling today.

Philosophic Understanding

The next major system upgrade available for our brains in our culture is tied up with the adoption of general, abstract, theoretic thinking. Certainly, younger students use abstract ideas, form generalizations, and grasp and frame theories, but with the mental upgrade to "philosophic understanding" these forms of thought take on a new and central importance, shifting the bias of the mind toward locating the most significant meanings in theoretic abstract terms.

At the end of the first year of my B.A. in history, in a social gathering of our small cohort, Dr. Bossy asked us to identify the most important thing we had learned during the year. When it came to my turn I said, "Anglo-Saxon law." I was told that the question referred to life in general not the content of the courses we had taken. I mumbled a bit incoherently that I really did mean Anglo-Saxon law because I had become fascinated by how one group of people used means of persuasion, coercion, and control to generate order in society, particularly an order that benefited them. I tried to explain how details of the imposition of law in Anglo-Saxon kingdoms connected with the experiences I had been having as a novice in student politics, discovering how the more adept "politicians" managed to manipulate rules of order, motions, and allies to get their way. After I had stumbled around unclearly for a few minutes, Dr. Bossy said, "You mean you've discovered power." He was exactly right. What had earlier been a lot of detailed, varied, and disparate pieces of knowledge and experience had become swept together into generalized concepts in which I had begun to locate their real meaning; those diverse and different facts and events were really just aspects of that great new vivid concept "power" and the processes by which it operated. It wasn't that I hadn't understood the meaning of *power* before, but it had come into a new focus with a new intellectual potency, generating a new kind of understanding. When I now looked at political events in Indonesia or the drama of French or American elections, I had a new and potent tool available for analyzing and understanding them. They were no longer just particular and distinct events — Anglo-Saxon law, student politics, American elections, and even family relationships were all phenomena that could be now understood in terms of the uses and abuses of power. And, of course, power wasn't the only concept I was coming to understand in this way — ideas about nature, society, love, evolution, psychology, and so on, began to populate and form my new mental landscape. "Philosophic understanding" is constituted by the development of a range of such concepts and the sense that they expose the real *truth* and the *real* reality of things. Before the emergence of these powerful concepts, we feel, we had seen as through a glass darkly.

Another way to recognize this somewhat distinctive kind of understanding might come from remembering those word problems with which math textbook writers persecuted us. If five men took two and a half hours to dig twelve holes, how many hours would it take eight nuns to . . . no, no . . . sorry, I got a bit mixed up there, as I usually did with such problems at school. I used to worry about whether it was winter or summer or how a few bars of chocolate might influence productivity, and what were the holes for anyway, and if they were to hit some really big stones . . . Time up! Test over! Flunked again. These word problems are very ancient in the teaching of mathematics (Gerofsky, 2004) and have been used for millennia to try to ease students into a new kind of thinking. For the math problem to be solved, it didn't matter whether it was men, nuns, or emus digging the holes, and it didn't matter that digging was going on or that holes were the products of the irrelevant digging. To solve such problems, imagining the situation described was a distraction. Yet what we would like to do, faced by such a problem, is find a crew of five men who would dig twelve holes in two and a half hours and then stand, stopwatch in hand, and time how long it took three of them to dig seven holes—or whatever the problem demanded. But the point of the exercise is to abstract our thinking from this "analog" world, focus only on the relevant numbers, and perform the appropriate calculations.

Mathematics, and the sciences, are areas where such abstract thinking is used remorselessly, but we can think in this manner about anything. The "philosophic" upgrade is constituted by the generation of a conceptual world, made up of general ideas, that derives from but is different from the everyday world of particular things and events. This theoretic conceptual world is a bit odd and insubstantial; it is insecure and in need of constant support, not being a kind of thinking most of us engage in without some effort. It seems to occur systematically only when there is a community consistently supporting it, such as a university. The difficulty of sustained "philosophic" or theoretic, abstract thinking is indicated by the small proportion of adults who can manage more than the most basic mathematics or grasp scientific ideas of any complexity. For those who become fluent in its use, however, it provides a tool kit of wide utility and power. That few people achieve this level of thinking with fluency has led some who do and are not sympathetic to those less well equipped with philosophic cognitive tools to observe that "the bulk of mankind is as well qualified for flying as thinking" (Swift, 1801, p. 188).

Another example that might help identify "philosophic" thinking is evident in the difference between a "romantic" description of place—

in which the main sites, the most exotic scenery, the finest architecture are represented—and the "philosophic" abstraction from the
particulars that yields a map. Maps lack all "real" particularities, expressing them through symbols, but they are nevertheless invaluable
for finding one's way about. (One can often find "romanticized" maps
of villages or small towns, in which, instead of symbols, there are
miniaturized pictures of the streets and buildings, as though one is
looking down at an angle from half a mile up. We typically find such
maps very satisfying—we can gain the "philosophic" advantage without having to make the effort of "philosophic" thinking. We get this
"romantic" satisfaction also from model train systems and from mini-
ature towns and villages we can walk giantly through.)

Now, for some reason, it isn't easy to describe abstract, theoretic
cognitive tools without using abstract, theoretic language—which, as
we've seen suggested, can require some effort and be a bit of a slog. So
here we go:

This new abstract theoretic world can come to appear more real
and reliable than the everyday particular world from which it is abstracted. Our senses and our feelings can deceive us, as becomes
evident when we look at the astonishingly divergent accounts wit-
nesses commonly give of the same event. Our theoretic world can
thus seem to be more "objective." (We might feel that the castle is
further north and not so far, but what we feel is irrelevant compared
to where the reliable map says it is. The photograph's evidence that
you wore a green dress to the interview cannot be refuted by your
memory of having worn a Spiderman outfit.) The transition to this
new kind of thinking can be very exciting for students who access it
quickly and thoroughly. They believe that they are at last able to
understand how things truly are and how the world really works. The
world thus becomes re-seen as made up of vast processes—historical,
social, psychological, anthropological—governed by laws and rules
that abstract, theoretic thinking alone can discover.

What had been houses and buses and shops and people and politics
and money and so on becomes "society." And the current state of
society can be thought of as "postindustrial," "narcissistic," "alienat-

ing," "multicommunitied," "cyberspacial," or whatever—and these stratospheric generalizations are seen as meaningful. Such a state of society, in turn, can be fitted into historical schemes, in which "progress" is evident, or "decline," or "cyclical chaos," or "going to hell in a handcart." The danger in the adoption of this tool kit is in becoming so intoxicated with its abstractions and their manipulation that one loses touch with "reality," (another of those grand generalizations whose particularity can get lost). That is, in one of those unfortunate old human equations, increased power entails increased risk.

One common problem is that students can develop excessive confidence in their generalizations, patterns, theories, ideological and metaphysical schemes, and the other inhabitants of the abstracted realm. We see the victims of this danger all around us—the convinced, the dogmatic, the certain—and each of us is likely to become one of these victims if we aren't careful, and even if we are. The excessive conviction that is a danger of immature philosophic understanding seems even to be an advantage in modern politics, appearing as the passionate intensity we might sensibly be wary of. But the great gift of "philosophic" thinking is that it enhances the brain's capacity for creating order in complexity, for seeing patterns within variety, for generating theories that account for events, things, and behavior. It can deliver a much more powerful mind to those who develop its cognitive tools.

So what are the cognitive tools of philosophic understanding? One of the constituent cognitive tools that comes along with this new "philosophic" tool kit involves the students' ability to see themselves as agents in the vast processes they have come to recognize. Their very sense of their own identity shifts as they begin to discard or distrust the "romantic" associations that had earlier contributed to their sense of self, and instead they recognize themselves as constructed by these vast historical, social, and so on, processes of which they are a part. They are who they think themselves to be, not as a product of their association with heroes, but because they have been born at a particular time and place within particular social conditions.

Using the romantic operating system, students were a bit like tourists, attending to the heroic and the exciting and exotic bits of the world past and present. But once the philosophic system takes hold, they become caught up in the great theoretical processes they are learning about. They become agents — directed by their theories of history and society to behave in particular ways, and directed by their ideology to take what steps they should to improve society. It gives a person a sense of direction, of belonging, and of purpose.

The cognitive tool that can carry the mind to increasingly sophisticated theoretic thinking is openness to anomalies. It works something like this: Early in their engagement with theoretic thinking, students are attracted to powerful general ideas that suddenly sweep together a whole range of phenomena and give a new perspective on them — as in the examples of "power" and "society" above. Similarly students become engaged by general theories. Once the philosophic process is under way, and if students are intellectually inquisitive — which they will be if they have developed adequate degrees of somatic, mythic, and romantic understanding — they will come to recognize that the generalized concepts and theories are not adequate to the particulars they have swept together.

For example, exposed to a particular environment, a student might conclude that a competitive social and economic system will ensure that the best rewards will go to the best people and, so incentivized, such a system will be in the best interests of everyone in the end. But this student will then come across cases that don't fit this simple ideology; some poor and powerless people will be recognized as being in such a social condition as a result of bad luck rather than incompetence. These cases are anomalies to the neat ideological scheme. As the student gets to know some stupid and horrible rich people whose power and wealth are also a matter of luck, further anomalies will occur to the neat scheme.

The response to anomalies, usually, is not to discard the ideology but rather to adjust it only enough to accommodate the cases that don't fit. In the above example, the student might accept that, given regrettable inefficiencies in complex social systems, there will always be these chance casualties or unmeritorious beneficiaries, and that we should introduce mechanisms to minimize their occurrence or alleviate the stresses they cause to the system. That is, recognizing anomalies drives the ideology or generalization or theory to greater sophistication to better represent the particulars it is abstracted from. (Some people, of course, simply refuse to acknowledge anomalies, and so their schemes, ideologies, theories, and generalizations remain crude and inadequate for understanding or sensible behavior. Consider the ideologues of the Nazi Party or of Soviet Russia or of that guy on the talk show or of that history professor.) The more-sophisticated form of the ideology will then be open to further anomalies, which, in turn, the so-far well-educated student will accommodate by adjusting the ideology further. And, in turn again, the yet-more-sophisticated ideology will be open to yet further anomalies. And so it can go on, anomalies demanding greater sophistication, and greater sophistication bringing to light further anomalies. In the end, if all goes well educationally, the student comes to recognize that the ideology cannot be true or false or real in the way the particulars from which it is abstracted are.

Recognizing the interaction between generalizations, theories, ideologies, schemes, and so forth, and anomalies can lead quite directly to at least one teaching strategy for students developing philosophic understanding: the teacher encourages the development of theories and ideologies and then proposes to the student an anomaly, kicking the process into action. The teacher's role is not to try immediately to undermine the student's theory or ideology but rather to bring it to greater and greater sophistication, until it eventually crumbles under the load of anomalies, letting the student not only see the limitation of such generalized schemes but also recognize their utility and the circumstances in which they are genuinely powerful aids to effective thinking.

Another cognitive tool in the philosophic tool kit is the ability to form metanarratives. As stories help us to organize facts and events into emotionally meaningful patterns, so metanarratives help us to organize generalizations, theories, metaphysical schemes, ideologies, and other abstract conceptions into emotionally meaningful patterns.

In the above example of the student developing a crude ideology in which reliance on market forces was seen as inevitably leading to a better and richer society for all, that position would be supported by organizing data about past economic performances in particular situations into economic theories and calling on supportive anecdotal evidence, adding in a conviction about the sentimentality and unjustified optimism of opponents' claims and theories and generally lining up more or less efficiently an array of supports for the ideology. The efficiency with which we can locate supporting facts, events, theories, and so on, is not due to simply cautious calculation. Our emotional feelers, as it were, hunt with alert sensitivity for facts or events that have the right flavor or emotional sympathy — our neoconservative student, for example, will be especially alert to cases in which state subsidies proved ineffective, or in which entrepreneurial activity led to wealth for many. Also the student who constructs that kind of economic theory will also very likely take a predictable set of stances on a wide range of other issues, for example, concerning society's use of the death penalty, abortion, and school policies. What binds these stances — and other theories, metaphysical schemes, and so on — together is a metanarrative. It is a very general, and very powerful, tool that prominently uses our emotions to create coherent responses to varied phenomena. Metanarratives are clearly tied to complex higher psychological processes, and their purpose is to create for us emotional satisfaction with regard to the complex mental entities that inhabit our abstract realm. Like all of our tools, we may misuse it or not develop it very adequately. But its proper use allows us great facility in bringing together in emotional harmony an array of abstractions.

Metanarratives have been unpopular beasts of late, especially when they have been recognized only in their debased and unsophisticated forms — such as in the construction of male-female differences as part of a metanarrative of active domination and passive submission which in turn becomes tied into social and economic theories. "Philosophic" thinking came to a kind of maturity in the Enlightenment project — in which reason and calculation were brought to bear on the social, physical, psychological, and historical problems that beset us. Because many Enlightenment thinkers announced their project as being in contrast to the undisciplined, emotional, mythic, impressionistic, poetic thinking that preceded their entry to the intellectual state, "philosophic" forms of thinking have tended to be seen as bloodless, overly rational, calculative, and dry. The methodologies of the sciences, for example, seem designed to remove anything connected with human values and emotions from their operations. Yet the use of the metanarrative tool is to engage our emotions with our abstract, theoretic thinking appropriately.

That "appropriately" is the hard part, of course. A proper use of our metanarrative tool will not lead to determining our experimental methods by how we feel that day, or constructing our economic theories based on our self-interest, or devising cosmologies on the basis of what would be most comforting, or forming ideologies on the basis of our emotional responses to the activities of a few members of an identifiable group of people, or any similar injection of emotion or value into our theory construction or calculations. If we do see examples of the above it is due to inappropriate uses of metanarratives. The appropriate use is to enlist and enrich our emotional engagement in the pursuit of understanding, to recognize the social dimensions of the products of our inquiries and research, to keep proportionate human values in mind as directors of our inquiries and framers of policy, and to embed particular discoveries into wider contexts that shape their meaning. That is, while scientific research might seem, at some level, properly value free, an appropriate use of metanarratives would influence the choice of topic to explore and the expectation of uses for the resulting knowledge, the scientist's hopes and fears would guide decisions, the passion to know would dictate the pace of the work, and the meaning of the results would be made more complex by being fitted to value-rich metanarrative contexts.

A conservationist metanarrative, for example, could direct a scientist who holds it to focus on the issue of global warming, and especially to locate as a topic of research something that might provide important evidence for or against some claim about climate change being due to human activity. The metanarrative would not influence the research itself, but would stand alert, as it were, guiding the scientist to the problem and further guiding the way the results could be interpreted and disseminated. Without such metanarratives, no field of research would likely make any progress, and it is hard to imagine how science itself would have developed. Similarly, all fields of inquiry that draw on the tools of abstract, theoretic thinking require metanarratives to set their work in contexts of wider human meaning.

Another related philosophic tool is the drive for some bedrock of truth, reality, reliability, authority, or certainty. This, too, is subject to disapproval, suspicion, sidelong glances, and distrust by many today. It, too, is seen as part of the Enlightenment project that led to over-confident claims to have located truth in self-interested social, political, and religious movements. The drive to sort out knowledge into more reliable forms than existed in societies where dogma was un-questionable led to our modern world of energetic inquiry. While many of the products of this search for authority have been questioned, other products—like dictionaries, encyclopedias, textbooks—are accepted as important sources of authority, though subject to revision and correction, like any theoretical and abstract account of the world. Even if some ideal, absolute certainty is inaccessible to us, claims that can be made with greater confidence than others can be sorted out. The fact that we can't be sure how our universe developed doesn't mean that the Big Bang theory has to take equal status with the claim that the universe was made—with our memories and all—ten minutes ago by Puff the Magic Dragon. The "philosophic" search for security and authority keeps intellectual inquiry constantly alert, giving it both energy and a sense of direction.

Imagine you are standing on a bank of the Windrush River on a summer morning. Your somatic tool kit might incline your mind to become caught up with the slow and sinuous movement of the reeds in the current and feel the strong tranquility they somehow communicate. Your mythic tool kit might incline your mind to become caught up by the river's eternal flow and to see its water supporting the grasses and trees, the animals, insects, and fish against drought and death.

Your romantic tool kit might incline your mind to become caught up by this ideal pastoral scene of exquisite beauty which you determine to defend against encroaching housing, shops, and factories and their effluent. And your philosophic tool kit might incline your mind to consider the quantity of water and its distant sources, and perhaps wonder why it maintains so strong a flow after weeks without significant rain or why the water doesn't seep away into the ground, or to consider whether one might dam such a river to generate power — though perhaps the flow is too small and not steep enough and the land is too flat beside it — or whether it would be useful, and cheap in energy, to use it as a one-way transportation route, perhaps for sending logs downstream — though it might have too many sharp bends or shallows to avoid constant logjams, and anyway, there might not be a good source of lumber upstream, though one might buy land for a tree farm on such a bank as this. Or, as you reach down and lift out a cool handful of water, you might reflect on the tiny pool in your hand and realize it is no longer a part of the river, but as you let it dribble through your fingers, each drop rejoins the near-infinite number of drops to become again the ever-changing always-the-same river, into the same instantiation of which you cannot step or dip your hand twice, as it eases its way from here to the sea, to the clouds, to the rain, to this or some other river, passing through plants and us, in a recurrent cycle that keeps the Windrush meandering for ever, for now.

Ironic Understanding

The final upgrade for our brains currently available in our culture is the tool kit of irony. Irony? In its simplest form irony is recognized in the difference between what is said and what is meant. "It's springtime! Oh joy! Around again comes the delight of doing taxes." "Those Ku Klux Klan guys sure have a great sense of rhythm." "What's the news? The world is grown honest." "He has occasional flashes of silence that make his conversation perfectly delightful." Or, most simply, "Hitler was a saint, Casanova was chaste, and the Marquis de Sade was reticent." That is, the reader knows the writer does not intend these statements to be understood literally. So the reader is being invited to search for a meaning other than the overt or literal meaning.

Ironic understanding is the recognition not only that language can be used to mean the opposite of, or something radically different from, what is actually stated, but that there is *always* some difference between what we mean and what *can* be put into language. The person who develops ironic understanding is constantly aware of the limits of words. It is Flaubert's contrast between our desire to move the stars to pity and our discovery that all we can actually do with language, however hard we try, is something more like beating out tunes on a honk-tonk for bears to dance to. Language grows out of our bodily activity in our early years, but there is always a distance between our experience, feelings, somatic understanding, and what we can express in words. Words are solids, experience is liquid.

This rather complicated recognition of the gap between meaning and the ability of language to express and communicate meaning is at the heart of ironic understanding. Like each of these tool kits, forms of irony appear earlier. Young children know that they can't always express in words what they feel, and throughout the development of the different kinds of understanding most people recognize this fairly obvious fact. Irony can be used in any earlier kind of understanding, and some people develop a delight in ironic humor. What is distinctive about the ironic recognition of limits on language is a profound realization that all the beliefs, ideas, "truths," facts, and everything else expressed in language suffer from a systematic inadequacy to the phenomena the words are supposed to represent. Irony goes all the way down.

Now calling it an inadequacy is possibly misleading. We recognize that language is "inadequate" to some of the purposes we earlier felt it could perform for us. But our recognition also liberates us from earlier confusions and lets us see more clearly just what we can expect of language. In turn, this recognition opens up yet further purposes and pleasures that language can provide.

It is very easy to miss the implications of what may seem a simple recognition of the difference between what is said and what is meant.

One of the general implications results from the way the generalization/anomaly interaction described in the previous section fades away. The search for increasingly sophisticated generalizations and theories to account for anomalies can often be an intense driver of inquiry. In some fields, like the physical sciences, developing an adequate account of phenomena is the only game in town. Irony may seem to have nothing to do with the scientific business of stretching the language of number to capture general truths about the way things are. But once irony is developed it spreads like a dye through the whole fabric of the mind, while leaving many of the mind's features with all their characteristics still intact. How?

Well, irony's tool kit prominently involves a flexibility tool. One of its uses is to recognize that each of the earlier kinds of understanding had something distinctive to offer to an adequate view of anything. There is a tendency with the development of, say, romantic understanding to dismiss the tools of mythic understanding as childish or confused — the tendency to see things in oppositions is considered simplistic, the acceptance of fantasy figures like Santa Claus or the tooth fairy becomes shameful. Time to pack away the giants and witches and get on with real life. Similarly, there is a tendency with the development of, say, philosophic understanding to dismiss romantic tools as trivial and embarrassing — that association with heroes is considered pathetic, the energy that was expended on collecting stamps or shells seems incomprehensible and wasted, the fascination with the exotic and weird seems itself weird and exotic and something that is remembered with a vague shame.

What irony does is release us from the focus on the inadequacies of earlier kinds of understanding and instead enable us to recognize the contributions each kind of understanding can make. Ironic understanding recognizes the foundational importance of the body and its emotions in all our sense making, and the importance of the story-structuring and emotion-orienting tools of mythic understanding that we can deploy, and the importance of the energizing tools that engage us with reality and enable us to recognize the human dimensions of knowledge that come along with romantic understanding, and the importance of the philosophic searching tools that bring order and pattern to our understanding. ("All which thy child's mistake / Fancies as lost, I have stored for thee at home . . ." as Francis Thompson put it in "The Hound of Heaven.")

We make progress in ironic understanding as we develop greater appreciation of the contribution to our sense making of each of the previous kinds of understanding. We also can develop greater flexibility in deploying whichever kind of understanding is most appropriate for whatever mental task we face, and we can develop the ability to deploy any subset of them or all of them together in making richer sense of anything we see in the world and encounter in experience. The ironist who might sit upon that bank of the Windrush River would not be confined to any of the perspectives described but could use all of them. Irony is that multiperspectival congregation of views in the one mind at the one time. It's an intellectual homecoming.

Perhaps my metaphor of tools in a tool kit comes under increasing strain if I describe another of irony's contributions as a great lubricant of our mental flexibility by means of a new form of the tool of humor. The ability to move easily among kinds of understanding, and particularly to recognize the limitations on our philosophic schemes, yields a kind of intellectual playfulness. What is often a humorless and sometimes grim philosophic search for certainty gives way to a calmer recognition that while greater security of knowledge is desirable, the kind of certainty previously sought about general schemes is an epistemological confusion. In its place comes a sense of the great game of ideas and the delights this game can yield. The ironist is not going to hang or burn people or starve populations through a lack of the imagination that comes with irony's recognition that ideologies or metaphysical schemes are products of an intellectual-ordering tool kit out of control. The controller, the modulating tool of our mature intellectual life, is irony.

What is one to make of schools of thought which proclaim that it is certainly true that there are no certain truths? And that on such a self-refuting basis the Enlightenment project is declared dead? Well, the ironist tends to giggle quietly and leave them to it. But the educator who wants to describe a path from infancy's exploration of the body's senses and sense making to ironic understanding has to draw heavily on the philosophic tools so well developed in the Enlightenment project. An ironist can sigh about the simplicity and crudity and endless inadequacies of a scheme of mutually enfolding kinds of understanding, but also recognizes that it's the best this particular ironist can do with the pitiful tools available to him.

Conclusion

In the previous chapter I provided a somewhat crude analysis of the main ideas I have been able to discern influencing education. In general, each of these ideas has contributed something important to educational thinking, but it requires large-scale blinders to conclude that we have managed to work out how to educate children well. This chapter, and its unfamiliar somatic, mythic, romantic, philosophic, and ironic kinds of understanding has resulted from thinking about the human mind differently from the way it has figured in the previous main educational ideas. Here the mind is conceived as an ambivalent thing, made up of culture drawn from outside the organism and of cognition within. So far, of course, everyone goes. The somewhat novel move here has been to locate a category that captures the ambivalence of mind — what I have been calling, not entirely satisfactorily, the cognitive tool. In general, the kind of category I am trying to frame for a richer educational scheme is one that combines epistemological, psychological, and emotional characteristics together.

In the past, especially since Rousseau's time, and more especially during the previous century, educational thinkers have focused on cognition or on knowledge separately and then typically inferred a role for the other. So those who have focused on cognitive development obviously recognized that knowledge was necessary to keep the process going, just as food was important for the body. *How* they came together, however, and which had precedence in determining or shaping the other, was never really worked out except as an assertion that on the one hand, knowledge would have to be selected to fit the priorities of cognitive development, or that on the other, the nature of knowledge drove cognitive development. For example, when laying out the place of knowledge vis-à-vis the student's individual developmental process, John Dewey argued that most basic is "recognition of the natural course of development" (1966, p.114), and as for curriculum knowledge: "The law for presenting and treating material is the law implicit in the child's own nature" (1897, p. 72). This follows his basic principle: "I believe that this educational process has two sides — one psychological and the other sociological; and that neither can be subordinated to the other or neglected without evil results following. Of these two sides, the psychological is the basis" (1897, p. 77). "Education, therefore, must begin with a psychological insight into the child's capacities, interests, and habits. It must be controlled at every point by reference to these same considerations" (p. 78). Jean Piaget became influential in North American education when it became clear that his general views fitted well with Dewey's. In Piaget's view, the job of the school was to understand "the child's spontaneous development, which it should reinforce by adequate methods instead of inhibiting it as it often does" (1961, p. 11). His theory in general aimed to describe "the natural psychological reality in terms of which we must understand the development of knowledge" (1964, p. 9).

Those who doubt this spontaneous developmental process even occurs are unlikely to allow that it should be reinforced by the curriculum and methods of teaching. Those who are "inclined to doubt that there is such a thing as cognitive development in the sense that developmental cognitive psychologists have in mind" (Fodor, 1985, p. 35) are more likely to assert that there "is no internal schedule of [cognitive] maturation that parallels the internally driven schedule of physical development" (Harré, 1990, p. xii). The educational objection is that it "is not that the mind is some kind of organ or muscle with its own inbuilt forms of operation, which if somehow developed, naturally lead to different kinds of knowledge" (Hirst, 1974, p. 40). What we require, instead, is an "education whose definition and justification are based on the significance of knowledge itself" (Hirst, 1974, p. 32).

This division between whether cognitive development or knowledge should have priority in shaping students' educational experience has driven educational thinking since Rousseau invented the problem for us. Those who give priority to knowledge in their blending we have commonly called "traditionalists"; those who give priority to cognitive development we have commonly called "progressivists." Neither has done a satisfactory job of delivering schools that educate well—for reasons discussed in the previous chapter. We can dispose of the stale arguments that have driven education for so long by disposing of their source—in a "plague on both your houses" response. Or rather, as both have contributed valuable insights about education, a more tempered response might be appropriate. But we cannot expect either of these conflicting positions to finally get it right. The general response that "Well, if one favors prioritizing knowledge and the other cognitive development, and we know both are important, we will simply balance both" won't work. In politics it would work to seek a centrist position between hard left and hard right. And, of course, there is an element of that commonsense response that is appropriate about education. It isn't, after all, like establishing the truth or otherwise of a scientific theory. But education is somewhere between these kinds of human activities. It isn't as open to negotiation as politics nor as closed as science. But we can imagine a conception of education that might gain the acceptance of a broad array of people—though it would have to be a conception that offered a way of achieving the ideals of both progressivists and traditionalists, in a form both might sign on to. Well, that's what I'm after here, so let's see how our move to "cognitive tool" talk, with its epistemological, psychological, and emotional components bound up together, might help articulate a new conception of schooling. It has so far given us a way of talking about education that doesn't seem offensive to either progressivists or traditionalists, so let's push on and see how many people stay on board.

A FIFTY-YEAR PROGRAM OF EDUCATIONAL REFORM:
2010–2060

The historian in the Sirius system whom we met in chapter 1 was going to describe how the public schools that were founded in the mid-nineteenth century were radically changed during the first half of the twenty-first century. What I would like to do in part 2 of this book is write that future history.

The first premise on which this fantasy is based is that the analysis of the modern school's problems in chapter 2 is generally correct. The second premise is that the outline of how minds can be better educated given in chapter 3 is also generally correct. The rest of this book, then, is an account of how we could gradually change the schools we have now to educational institutions that avoid the problems described in chapter 2 and incorporate the ideas described in chapter 3. I will lay out, in five chapters, how we can get from here to there. Each chapter will cover a ten-year period.

In each of the following chapters I will focus on changes in teaching, in the curriculum, and more generally in the institution of the school. I don't anticipate that these will change at an equal pace. In the first ten years, for example, I will indicate a number of changes in teaching, but I expect hardly any impact on the curriculum or on the institution of the school itself. The proportion of attention to these three foci will shift in the subsequent chapters. In general I will describe how, step by step, decade by decade, a practical program of gradual reforms will deliver more effective educational institutions and practices. And, of course, the distinctions among teaching, the curriculum, and the school are hardly very sharp, as changes to any one will also involve changes to the others in most cases. But I'll use them, on the understanding that they are a convenience and not to be taken as rigidly distinct categories.

You might reasonably conclude that this is a utopian fantasy. *Utopia* was Sir and Saint (not a frequent combination in British history) Thomas More's word for his imagined society. It is commonly assumed that the word is a compound of the Greek words *ou* and *topos*, signifying "no place." But it seems at least as likely that More had in mind *eu + topos* (a well or happy place) or *eus + topos* (a good place). So, in the less usual sense, yes, this is intended as a "eutopian" view of the school and how we can make it an educationally well and good place. (Oscar Wilde suggested that a world map that didn't include Utopia wasn't worth looking at.)

When an institution of great complexity and importance, such as the school, becomes intricately bound up with nearly all other social institutions, attempting to bring about significant changes will meet a multitude of resistances. Some initial reforms may be allowed and even encouraged, but if they expand and threaten to cause deep and wide-scale changes, the institutions will then inexorably, link by link, tighten into an adamantine obstacle preventing any major reforms. Or, at least, that's what they say. But significant changes do occur in institutions, so let's see how plausible we can make this trek towards an educational "eutopia."

There may be some meanly skeptical readers who will doubt my prophetic access to the great database about the future. Perhaps I can offer this history of the future to such people more prosaically, as simply a device to demonstrate the practical implications of the ideas sketched in part 1.

Where are we now with regard to the ideas that are set, at least in this account, to transform education? What is the preliminary state of play before the official kickoff year of 2010? I confess it doesn't look very promising. There are a few books and articles that give theoretical background (esp. Egan, 1997) and a few that describe how the theory can be put into teaching practice (e.g., Egan, 2005, 2006). There is also an active but small research group and webpage (www .ierg.net), with some co-researchers in a dozen or so countries and a couple of thousand or so teachers, administrators, and college and university instructors with varying degrees of commitment to furthering the impact of these ideas within educational institutions—if they can only work out precisely what these ideas and their implications are.

But the world of education is full of such groups, proposing particular reform agendas, driven by particular ideas, and in many cases (but unlike this case) energized by charismatic leaders. Most of these groups are trying to implement some aspects of the general progressivist program (e.g., Project Zero—www.pz.harvard.edu), with a smaller number trying to refine and make more attractive the traditional program (e.g., Core Knowledge—www.coreknowledge.org). Both of the examples cited have significant funding and many thousand committed proponents; they have produced widely used curriculum materials, run well-attended conferences and workshops, established prolific publishing programs, and there are thousands of schools internationally implementing their ideas. In the educational pond these are large fish, and yet I am proposing that a tiny tadpole will make a bigger splash within the next fifty years or so.

How easy to roll out the David and Goliath scenario, with its unlikely and delightful conclusion. But the progressivist and traditionalist champions are on familiar territory, and the educational world understands their aims and language. To most people in education, the ideas of what we have come to call "imaginative education" are a bit odd. The aims and language of progressivism largely hold the field — even if getting those aims into practice remains a problem — and the main traditionalist contenders can also count on long familiarity. Taking on a significantly different paradigm is much harder than working with "normal," familiar educational ideas. (One common response to the unfamiliar is to distort it till it looks like something familiar, and this will be a part of the problem that will detain the revolution a tad.) Hence the fifty-year saga. Well, let's see if I can describe a scenario you will find plausible in which these new ideas can significantly transform education in the years to come.

What follows, then, is supposed to be an extract from the book written by our historian on the fifth planet of Sirius, two and a half thousand years in the future, as she grappled with the radical changes in schooling in the first part of the twenty-first century.

Teaching: 2010–2020

One of the major influences in education in the second decade of the twenty-first century resulted from the fortunes of movements connected with "scientific" or "evidence-based" "best-practices," with "high-stakes testing" procedures, and the push for greater control and accountability in order to drive up students' test scores in literacy, numeracy, and science in particular. National prestige was increasingly tied to the scores achieved in international assessments, and when the students of some countries that spent vastly more per capita on education performed worse than those of many relatively impoverished countries there was increasing pressure from parents and politicians on schools to do better. The more advanced and successful economies also needed increasingly skilled workers, able to support and extend the technological developments of the time and also expand the "knowledge economy," which had become a crux of international competition.

What became apparent during the first years of this decade, from about 2010 to 2013, was that the "science-based" procedures developed and implemented very widely during the first decade of the twenty-first century could indeed have beneficial effects on literacy and other scores. But people faced the puzzle of there also being a strong positive correlation between those improved scores and students' dwindling interest in the areas they were testing so well in. In the case of literacy this meant that as scores improved, students read less.

A special conference was convened in Singapore in 2014 to discuss the problem. Here is a report on the conference that appeared in the *Strait Times Interactive* the day after it ended. It features a lengthy interview with one of the more outspoken young education professors, Dr. Robertson Gill, whose book *What Hope for the School?* had recently become popular around the world:

The minister, Mei Pin Tao, opened the conference at the National University on September 23rd. Its purpose was to make recommendations to the minister and to the governments of the sponsoring countries about what has been called the "increasing scores, declining interest" problem. Educators came from thirty-four countries.

At the conclusion of the conference we spoke with Dr. Robertson Gill, a prominent educator from the University of Mumbai. Asked for his views about the success of the conference, he looked at our reporter for a moment and said, "Success? Same old, same old." He agreed to sit down in the Long Bar at Raffles and give a more lengthy analysis of the event.

STI: Why did you say, "Same old, same old"?

RG: I could have predicted all the positions and suggestions before I came. I'd hoped for some new suggestions, but heard only the old routines.

STI: Perhaps you could describe for our readers . . .?

RG: You have the old progressivists. Their line is that the neocon test-driven teaching allows no freedom or time for students to explore and learn in their own ways. So that makes the stuff they are learning boring to the kids. They see it, as do the teachers, as really pressured and dull work. So when not compelled to, they don't read. You've seen the collapse of publishing companies that didn't get into other media early. Your own newspaper is no longer a paper; it's all electronic, and mostly just a portal to audio and video news. The other line the progressivists push is that school has become even more dreary, test-driven, pressured, and like a work-house.

Then there are the standard traditionalists. They begin by denying the problem. It's only a *correlation* between increasing scores and less interest in the subjects, they say; the lack of interest isn't caused by the forms of testing. In general, they think the problem is that we don't have enough pressure, too many teachers aren't using the latest science-based procedures — mind you, we got that line from progressivists too. Tighter accountability, and all that. The cause of students' lack of interest in things academic for them is nothing to do with schooling. It's a simple result of the new media. Look, they keep saying, every kid has a roll-up screen in their back pocket, and for the cost of watching a few ads they can download to it any movie that's ever been made, any sports event that's ever been played, any concert, any TV show, "you-are-there" newscasts, and we don't need to mention the vivid porn. Everything has audio, so why do they need to read?

Did you hear the hand-wringers who attacked both sides from their "radical" position? The ones who talked about the sabre-toothed tigers?

STI: I didn't understand the reference.

RG: Well, in the mid-twentieth century the progressivists had a great rhetorical success (that's, by the way, the only kind you see in this business) talking about the "saber-toothed tiger" curriculum. This was an argument for junking the old traditional curriculum on the grounds that times and social conditions change and we must adapt to the new conditions. There's no point teaching — as the fable put it — all the nuances of hunting saber-toothed tigers if the tigers have moved away and now you are threatened by or need to eat mastodons. The progressivists who used this fable cast their traditionalist opponents — who wanted to preserve, say, Latin and the traditional literary canon — as not recognizing how the world had changed and how the old curriculum no longer served society's present needs.

The new form of this at the conference came from the tame radicals who said everything was just fine, even if kids aren't interested in reading or learning science. The hand-wringers who bewailed the declines in interest in reading, mathematics, and science were simply not keeping up with changes in society and technology. Reading was no longer so important a skill. They claimed that we are entering a new oral and technology-saturated culture, and educators should change teaching and curricula to fit the new world.

Not clear how we find the people to fix our roll-up computers, mind you. But they don't think that's a problem either.

STI: But perhaps you could explain why the improvements in test scores should have been discounted by so many educators at the conference?

RG: Well, the improvements weren't that great, of course, and they have plateaued, and the best bets are that they are in for steep declines — we see them going down already in some of the more advanced countries, ironically. The problem for them, of course, is that developing literacy, numeracy, and scientific skills is now a matter of national strategic importance. If they are to rely on us—I mean, India—to supply their advanced technology skills, that's not fair on us—we educate the kids and someone attracts them away with more money—and that will only encourage them to put off sensibly dealing with the problem even longer.

STI: Thank you, Dr. Gill.

Dr. Gill's prediction about declining test scores, especially in the more advanced societies proved true. As the decade came to an end, this debate about the causes of the decline in reading, the decline in interest in mathematics and science, and the precipitous decline in test scores in these subjects was by far the loudest part of the public debates about education.

In this context imaginative education (IE) began to have some success in limited areas of the overall education system. A number of small programs had been developed based on IE principles, and teachers reported that, whatever else IE did, it clearly engaged their students' emotions and imaginations in learning about the content of the curriculum. That is, one of its recognized strengths was precisely what was increasingly clearly recognized as a weakness in the education system as the decade went on. As teachers proclaimed these results, IE procedures were made the subject of the usual kinds of research studies, and a number of them showed very positive results. Some didn't, but the longer the period in which the students worked with IE materials and procedures the more likely they were to show positive results. Some of the results were quite dramatically positive, especially those with aboriginal students and inner-city students who had in the past commonly done poorly in schools.

But many new programs do well in such tests, so nothing much was generally read into them, especially by the main proponents of IE, who distrusted such testing anyway. But the results, published in various journals and books, were enough to generate more than fringe interest, and enough to make IE websites objects of many hits from teachers wanting to download their free materials. The increased attention to the basic theory of IE, and its account of how knowledge grows in the mind, was an incidental benefit of this new interest. The theoretical bases were quite at odds with those currently being emphasized in the schools, in particular IE's emphasis on the importance of the emotions, imagination, and humor for meaningful learning. While attractive to many teachers and professors of education, the unfamiliarity and, consequently, difficulty of the theory slowed its wider acceptance. During this period, outlines of the theory and examples of its practices began to appear in standard texts designed for teacher education programs.

At best, though, for the first half of the decade, the result of this small attention amounted only to scattered application of IE practices in schools. But those who used them successfully often became strong promoters, and there appeared a number of teacher networks that offered support to other teachers willing to give them a try.

One of the crucial stimuli to the spread of IE later in the decade was the development of IE teacher education modules. The Imaginative Education Research Group (IERG) designed, tried out, and then made widely available "resource modules" that could be used in teacher education programs to introduce the ideas to pre-service teachers and to demonstrate how the principles could be put into practice in the everyday classroom. The kit involved various print materials and CD-ROMs with lecture-demonstrations, slide presentations that the class instructor could use to introduce ideas and practices, and videos of the ideas being put into practice in schools. There was also ample support material for the students to try out the ideas in their own practice sessions in classes.

This became quite widely used as an elective in dozens, then a few hundred, teacher education programs. By the end of the decade it was available in maybe a tenth of the programs for teacher preparation across Europe and North America, and it was used by proponents of IE in many other countries. It might be best to describe this smaller module by seeing how a typical student experienced it.

The journal kept by a young woman, Sara Blenkins, who was enrolled in a teacher education program in a mid-American state university in 2016, will be used to describe the program. Sara was a bright and confident young woman who had done well at school and completed a good degree with joint majors in political science and history. She was preparing to become a primary-school teacher. In her program, there was the possibility of spending a two-week period of intensive work with one of a number of electives. Students who felt less confident about their management of the classroom could choose a mini-module that would focus on increasing those skills, or, similarly, on planning units of study, or on dealing with a multilingual classroom, or on working with particular conditions of handicap, or on use of voice and movement, or on a number of other topics. Because she had heard some good things said about the imaginative education mini-module by two friends of hers who had taken the program the previous year, Sara signed up for the IE elective. Here are some sections from her journal:

First day is always a bit clammy in any class. There are fifteen of us. Ten women. We did the usual introductions and were invited to account for why we were taking this module. "My friends liked it," was enough to get me by. Some of them, especially the keener-guy across the table, said they'd read a few books about it, a couple said their teachers had used it when they were at school, a couple just liked the description in the catalog, but mostly they said friends had recommended it. I noticed that most people in the group had done well in the earlier parts of the program, so I guess we were a group ready to take on a bit of a challenge.

The instructor was a woman from Georgia—the country not the state—and had a fairly thick accent, though she was clear enough. Bit of a dry sense of humor though she laughs a lot, which makes for a nice atmosphere. Leila Zhordania, and we were to call her Leila. I didn't find it easy. She was a tough woman.

Leila—I'm practicing!—began with an illustrated talk that was titled "A brief guide to imaginative education." She pointed out that she didn't want us to take notes for the time being, as our folders contained a booklet with all the information in it, along with a disc with the slides and a more detailed commentary, and we would be expected to review these later. Initially the talk about cognitive tools and tool kits left me less than turned on, reminding me of the technicist-sounding workshops I'd had on stating objectives as the first step of lesson planning.

But by the end of the class I really was interested in the idea that the main things I should be thinking of in planning a lesson were tied up with feelings and images, metaphors and jokes, rhyme and rhythm, stories and wonder, heroes and the exotic, hopes, fears, and passions, hobbies and collecting, narrative and oppositions, and a number of other "tools" I can't remember now. Certainly a step up from "objectives stated in performance terms as far as possible."

Leila said that the focus of the next few classes in the mini-module would be on showing how attention to hopes and fears, and so on, in planning and teaching can transform students' learning, both in terms of the pleasure and engagement the students get from learning and, not unconnectedly, in the amount they learn and their retention of it. I must say I was a bit skeptical about the last claims. Leila was clearly a major keener for this stuff.

Sara's skepticism was widely shared at the time. It is hard for people today to understand that in early twenty-first century discourse about education the imagination, human emotions, and humor were rarely mentioned. Instead, a central concept to their thinking about education was an astonishingly restricted sense of "learning," which mostly was seen as little more that memorizing the knowledge content of the curriculum. That knowledge without engagement of the imagination and the emotions was disconnected from human meaning seemed, bizarrely, of little evident concern in most educational research and literature. Educational success was assessed largely by how well an

attenuated form of knowledge was stored in the memory. Modern
people will no doubt wonder how this could ever have been considered to have anything much to do with education. But this is among
the presuppositions with which Sara writes. She continues:

> I mean, I enjoyed the presentation, and the ideas on the surface at least
> made a lot of sense, but when I thought about how they could be
> applied to teaching geometry or spelling or science absolutely nothing
> came to mind. I also worried a bit that I was being asked to become a
> kind of entertainer, with jokes and images, stories of heroes, and so on.
> I thought the main point of the lessons would get lost. Later when I was
> reviewing the materials, I got this slightly spooked sense that this ap-
> proach was somehow asking me to become a different kind of teacher
> from what I had been planning to become.

The second class began with Leila reviewing the cognitive tools of
"mythic understanding." We spent some time considering how to recognize them in our own thinking. She gave us some exercises to make
the tools clearer, and we worked on these in small groups — I got to be
with the keener from across the table, Kurt, who wasn't as bad as I'd
feared, and Marnie and Jessica. We discussed examples till it was clear
that everyone had a pretty good idea of what "mythic understanding"
consisted of, at least in some fairly general way. Leila suggested that we
spend some time later trying to come up with another tool we might
add to this set.

Then we got to play around with the first of the planning frameworks. At first glance it didn't look any step up on the objectives ones
we'd been given earlier. In fact this was more complicated. Leila described it as the simple framework and said that we'd spend a couple of
days working at it. Anyway, here's what we got:

Mythic Planning Framework
1. Locating importance
   What is emotionally engaging about the topic? How can it evoke
wonder? Why should it matter to us?
2. Thinking about the content in story form
   2.1. Finding binary opposites
      What binary concepts best capture the wonder and emotion of the
topic? If this were a story, what would the opposing forces be?
   2.2. Finding images, metaphors, and drama

What parts of the topic most dramatically embody the binary concepts? What image best captures that content and its dramatic contrast? What metaphors can be used to help understanding?

2.3. Structuring the body of the lesson or unit

How do we teach the content in story form? How can we shape the content so that it will have some emotional meaning? How can we best bring out that emotional meaning in a way that will engage the imagination?

3. Conclusion

How does the story end? How do we resolve the conflict set up between the binary opposites? How much do we explain to the students about the binary oppositions?

4. Evaluation

How can one know whether the topic has been understood, its importance grasped, and the content learned?

I saw in the booklet that there was a variety of other frameworks, some of which looked even more incomprehensible. Teaching about math should be easier than this! Leila suggested we see the framework as just a kind of structured reminder of some of the main cognitive tools that can be used to engage students' imaginations. She then asked us to choose a topic and try to deal with items 1 and 2.1 from the framework — identifying the importance of the topic and finding binary oppositions within it.

I remembered trying to teach a unit on calendar in my first in-class sessions, to grade 1 kids. They had seemed to enjoy it — I had a rhyme they learned, and we spent some time with a big floor decoration that showed the days and months. There was a dance to go with it, and a song, and a game, all of which were supposed to get them to learn calendar stuff easily. And in class they were all involved and could repeat the rhyme and learned the dance well and seemed to have a good sense of it all. I'd been really disappointed, though, a few days after the unit when, just to make conversation in the corridor, I'd asked Jan, one of my five-year-olds, what day it would be tomorrow.

"Wednesday!" he said.

"Today is Wednesday, Jan, so what day is tomorrow?"

He had thought for a while, and then, with a shrug, had smiled charmingly and loped off to lunch. Later, when I mentioned this to my sponsor-teacher, Hee-soon Li, she said not to worry; it usually took a whole year for most kids to remember the days, months, and so on. Hee-soon said she had been in despair about it early in her career, and still used the games and clapping routines and other techniques she had developed to try to get the children to remember calendar names and sequences. Later she discovered that nearly all teachers had the same experience. That had been a bit consoling, but not much.

"It seems as though it ought to be easier, but it just doesn't mean anything much to children at that age," Hee-soon had said. "You've probably read why in Piaget's work. They aren't developmentally ready. Anyway, others decide children's routines and activities for the day; the children don't reflect on some abstract sequencing of the calendar till later."

But I thought it really ought to be easier. So I elected to do Calendar for my mythic framework topic.

I had assumed that "finding importance" was easy, because without knowledge of the calendar, people would be in chaos. Finding binary opposites took a couple of minutes. I thought of day and night, then realized these had no emotional resonance, so I settled for chaos and order. Leila had given us a quarter of an hour for this task, but I was finished in three minutes, so I went on to do the rest of the questions, outlining a unit that was similar to the one I had taught recently, fitting it to the categories and questions of the framework. At the quarter-hour mark, when Leila asked to hear some of our answers, being a big mouth, I stupidly said I'd be happy to — because I did want to get some feedback. Do I wish I hadn't! I also told her I'd finished the whole unit outline, not just the first couple of questions. I'm blushing just remembering my perky attitude. I thought she was going to give me extra points or something.

Leila asked me to take the class through the unit plan I'd developed. After I finished I was happy to get a few murmured congratulations from some of them, including Kurt Keener, as I call him, across the table. Leila also said, "Well done," and asked,

"Why does the week have seven days?"

I think I had my mouth open for a moment while I thought.

"I've no idea," I had to say.

"Who is Friday named after? Who is August named after?"

"I don't . . . isn't Friday after a goddess? Is August a person? I don't know. A god?"

"Why are there twelve months in a year?"

Leila was careful to indicate that she wasn't being critical of the unit plan and that it was really excellent from a conventional point of view. Big consolation! I felt about an inch high, but I noticed no one else was able to answer the questions either when she opened them up to the rest of the class.

She really was nice about it, so I didn't walk away feeling embarrassed, but she did manage to suggest that I had missed the whole point of IE. Even though I had read the material I hadn't really escaped from "the determining ideas" — is what she called them — I'd come to the class with. The other consolation, as the class went on, was that I was hardly alone. I guess we'd all approached planning the way we'd learned it in our earlier classes. We thought about the content and how to organize it in the categories of whatever planning framework we had — it was kind of a puzzle we had to solve. We hadn't really begun by trying to "feel about the topic," as Leila put it. I guess I had produced what one of the other students called, criticizing a method he had seen in his teaching practice, a "happy clappy" lesson, which tried to make the children's experience pleasant but at the cost of trivializing the subject matter.

Thinking about the class, I began to realize that the criticism she so gently zapped us with pretty well was true of much of the first-grade teaching I have seen. My "homework" after that class, which was the same as everyone's, was to try again to answer items 1 and 2.1 from the framework, but taking it more seriously and discovering, in my case, what was important about the calendar.

I spent the rest of the day on the Internet, learning why there are seven days, and who the days are named after and who the months are named after, and much else. I confess — feeling a bit weird about it — that I stayed up late, fascinated. Why had no one ever taught me these things? By the time I went to bed I felt quite indignant that no one had taught me this really interesting stuff. I felt vaguely that I had been somehow cheated. I went to class the next day more humble, but with a better lesson plan.

We spent the next class rehearsing each student's answers to the first items of the framework. Leila was encouraging and constantly pushing us to find deeper meanings and more potent binary oppositions that captured those meanings. By the end of the class, I was quite exhausted. Finding emotional importance and wonder was hard work! It was certainly unlike anything I'd ever done before in my teacher ed program.

And that business of binary opposites, which had seemed easy at first, was really tough.

But I began to feel that while what Leila was pushing us to do was valuable stuff, this whole method was just too difficult. It couldn't catch on in general. It just asked too much of the teacher. Mostly, though, I felt unsure that I was "getting it," or that I was getting it right. The earlier talk about stories and jokes and images—and we hadn't started on images yet!—was attractive, but this hard and uncertain struggle was nothing like what I'd expected. I was a bit relieved to recall that my friends who took the mini-module last year had said it was tough to start with but well worth it. I decided to stick it out for a few more days.

Leila tried to assure us that there were no right answers to choosing binary opposites; it's just that some were more potent than others.

"I don't know what you mean by potent," one of the students said.

"Well, we can all make up fictional stories for children, but some are more powerfully engaging than others. Children are fascinated by some stories and ho-hum about others. That fascination is what I mean by potency. If you look at the best fictional stories for children of this age—the ones that engage children most powerfully—they have the same set of cognitive tools at work as a successful IE lesson. The planning framework is a kind of introduction to how to tell a good factual story. Making good fictional stories isn't easy, but the results can be magical. Similarly, learning IE procedures takes some work, but the return in children's learning more than repays the effort. Also, though this way of planning will seem a bit alien to begin with, quite quickly it will become intuitive. In many ways it is a more natural way to approach planning a lesson or unit—it encourages us to think of the curriculum as a set of wonderful true stories we have to tell children. In fact, as you may have discovered, it's really the way we would like to have been taught ourselves."

By the end of the first week I was getting the hang of those first two steps. Leila spent so much time on them, she said, because once we did that opening part well, everything else followed easily. My other lesson plans, and those of the other students, had indeed been easy to flesh out once we'd worked out the first steps. But working out those steps was still a struggle. We had to think hard! And often I had to spend hours searching for more information about topics. It wasn't that I was going to teach it all to children, but I had to do it sometimes to find out what were the most potent oppositions and images and metaphors to grab kids' imaginations. The other thing that became clear was that the more I knew about a topic the easier it was to become imaginatively engaged myself.

It is perhaps worth noting here something else that would astonish people today. Sara's self-identity as a teacher rested on a commitment to children, in some rather vague sense — almost a kind of subdued maternal feeling for them. It also was tied up with an expertise at managing a large group of children by means of skill at taking the knowledge in the curriculum and breaking it into classroom activities, calculating how to break it down into chunks that conformed to the time slots available in the school day. In addition, knowledge of children's developmental stages, learning styles, and so on, would also be a part of her self-identity as a teacher. If asked about how far her identity as a teacher turned on being an expert in the knowledge she was teaching, she would have been surprised. The elementary-school curriculum was not, in her view, or in that of her contemporary teachers, such that disciplinary expertise was called for in any significant degree. Knowing the children in depth was more important in her view than knowing the curriculum content in depth. If asked how far knowing how to engage the imaginations and emotions of her students was important, she would likely have agreed that it mattered, but it hadn't been something she had learned much about, and she would assume that was a matter of an individual teacher's intuition about such things. And if asked how far using a sense of humor and developing it in her students was an important component of a teacher's identity, she would likely have said that was a matter of personality, and not something everyone should be forced to do. I can say these things with some confidence, as they are described in other parts of her journal, to which we can return:

> During the last week of the mini-module we focused on setting up the story structure. I was a bit surprised that a couple of the students still felt they had to make up a fictional story somewhere in the lesson, despite the fact than Leila said again and again that these were factual stories, like the newspaper editor asking what's the story on the explosion in the docks. The editor isn't asking for a fiction but a shaping of

the events to bring out their emotional importance. The more the reporter can find out, the easier it is to find the "story line" and the particularly potent details that will bring out the drama and emotional importance. But in the end, most people got it, though I was surprised that some didn't, even Kurt Keener. He seemed so caught up with how well he'd learned everything in all his courses so far that the idea that what mattered now was feeling and imagining and generating emotionally charged images and even locating humor just seemed a bridge too far for him.

By the middle of the second week we'd lost four people. And a few others were clearly having serious difficulties—including Kurt, whose pride wouldn't let him ever drop a class, and he was determinedly trying to turn IE planning into something he could somehow find the right answers to if he just read enough, and to get an "A," even though the mini-modules weren't graded. I guess he wanted a virtual A. The rest of the class—maybe eight or nine of us, maybe ten, and maybe Clare will catch on in the end—was feeling some comfort and confidence using the framework, even though it remained difficult at times.

Leila complimented us, and then returned to the "brief guide" in order to pull back from the details of planning and consider the theory within which the framework existed. Like everyone else in the cohort, I had always thought educational theory basically boring. We had learned about the triumph of child-centered, progressivist ideas over the old traditionalist, teacher-centered ideas. We also had been told that progressivist ideas were still in some conflict with traditionalist practices in schools, and that the battle for progressivist practices had to be constantly fought. But I was beginning to recognize how IE was different from both of these sets of ideas and practices. Ironically, IE required even more emphasis on teaching a lot of knowledge than the traditionalist theory, and yet it was more child-centered than progressivism in its understanding of how knowledge grows in children's minds adequately only when their imaginations and emotions are engaged—at least, that was Leila's line, and I am beginning to think there's something to it.

At the conclusion of the mini-module I still felt a bit ambivalent about IE. I thought it was a useful addition to my skills as a teacher, and was also persuaded that it represented a somewhat new and distinct form of educating. But it wasn't easy. Or, at least, it was difficult if I didn't know much more about a topic than was in the school district's teachers' guides. When I knew a lot about a topic, it was quite easy to teach it in an IE way; the framework actually provided me with a way to hook into my own emotional engagement with a topic. I had become, I realized, quite excited by all the stuff I had been learning about the calendar in my spare hours, and could hardly wait to have a chance to teach it to a class next year.

Sara's ambivalence grew from her increasing realization during the second week of her mini-program on IE that she actually knew very little about the topics she was supposed to teach to children in grades 1 and 2. In the past she had just taken it for granted that the actual curriculum content was simple and basic and her work in the teacher education program was to understand children and help them adjust to school and each other and get across the simple content. Her mini-trauma, stimulated by Leila Zhordania's questions about why there were seven days in the week, had brought home to her how much better she would be equipped to teach such topics if only she herself knew a lot more about them. That is, one of the requirements of being able to stimulate children's imaginations was that she become better educated herself. She recognized, given that she wanted to be a teacher, that this wasn't something odd to expect, but it was something that no one else had brought up during her teacher education program.

Well, let's leave Sara and her ambivalences to take care of themselves. And we won't bother following Gregor, Sara's boyfriend, who enrolled in the secondary IE mini-module, through his two weeks' familiarization with its different set of cognitive tools and framework and his experiences with them. But both of them became teachers who used IE procedures quite commonly in their teaching and experienced results that surprised even them. They and thousands like them, over the years to the end of the decade, made IE moderately well known in regular public schools around the country. After a few years' experience they gave a number of workshops for fellow teachers, demonstrating how they had adopted and adapted IE and explaining why they thought it was so successful for them. They perhaps gave too much credit to IE and too little to their own energy and commitment, but this also helped the spread of IE into mainstream classrooms.

So, by 2020 IE procedures were being put into practice in hundreds, perhaps thousands, of schools by a fairly enthusiastic group of teachers. A dozen or so schools proclaimed themselves to be model "IE schools," and they became both test beds for developments in IE and sites commonly visited by those wanting to see the procedures at work. The increasing spread of knowledge about IE was a little deceptive, however. It became clear that many of the teachers who had been through the mini-module had instructors rather less acute than Leila Zhordania. Perhaps most teachers who planned on using one or another of the IE frameworks were actually preparing lessons a little like Sara's first attempt. They were doing straightforward progressivist teaching, using IE planning frameworks and language, but largely missing the spirit of the procedures. Most of these teachers had no sense of how they were failing to understand or implement IE.

To the historian it is commonly apparent that confusions are often more important than plans or intentions as causes of change. And it was certainly the case that fairly widespread confusion of IE with progressivist teaching methods was responsible for expanding information about IE. But this was not all confusion, of course, as both of these teaching methods did share a common cause in making the experience of students in schools and colleges and universities more meaningful. Both could be called child-centered programs, as they were sensitive to the learner and to changes in the ways students learned over time, and both tailored teaching to respond to the learner's needs. That they interpreted those needs differently, and saw the causes and kinds of changes in students' learning over time differently, was sometimes glossed over. IE benefited from the glossing and confusions as much as it did from the appeal of its own distinctive approach to educating.

The Curriculum: 2010–2020

A single sentence uttered at a conference in Salerno, Italy, in 2017 energized one of the more powerful influences on the curriculum in a century. The conference was sponsored by UNESCO in response to increasingly widespread dissatisfaction within universities with the academic quality of entering students, even though they came with good grades from their schools. "School grade inflation gone mad!" was one of the slogans in the publicity materials circulated to encourage academics to register. More than 3,000 leading scholars in the humanities, arts, and sciences were in attendance, and the subject of the conference was education. There was only a handful of invited professional educators present. The opening speaker had been a diplomat within the U.N. for many years, and then she had worked as head of UNESCO for the five years prior to the conference, which she had been responsible for convoking. She was Swedish.

She mounted the podium to give the opening address of the conference, and her first sentence was: "The school is the most anti-intellectual institution in our societies." Those who were present in the great hall later described how this assertion was greeted first by a moment of stunned silence, and then a spontaneous roar filled the hall from the delegates, and they were on their feet applauding and shouting for over three minutes. With a performer's sense of timing, recognizing that anything else she could say would only reduce the impact of that single sentence, she folded the sheets of the rest of her speech and walked calmly off the podium to the crowd's yet louder applause.

The rest of the conference gave way to an elaboration and analysis of her opening statement, involving spontaneous talks followed by intense discussions by delegates from around the world. The "Salerno movement" rapidly developed into an enormously powerful lobby of academics whose determined aim was to influence the curriculum of, and teaching at, the schools. There was much talk at the conference about the hostility of schools to intellectual life, as those scholars saw it. That such a characterization, or caricature, was unfair to very many successful schools and dedicated teachers was irrelevant to the way the sentence became a slogan, energizing a mass movement of largely middle-class parents and university teachers.

For the historian, such large movements, which develop from claims that on their face are absurd or largely meaningless, focus attention on the unpredictable nature of our subject. There are, of course, those who say the movement was not unpredictable, just that we attend too much to the surface causes and ignore or cannot see the greater underlying causes. In this case, what sense did it make to suggest that schools were more anti-intellectual than, say, banks or bottled-drinks companies? Yet, clearly the response from the audience in Salerno revealed vividly that those most concerned with the intellectual life of the time had come to see the public school as an enemy rather than the ally it ought to have been.

One aspect of the rise of progressivism was the schools' largely successful fight to have control of their curricula and to establish that their purpose was to prepare students for life, not for college and university. This success had been supported by the Eight-Year Study in the early 1930s. One of the largest educational research projects ever undertaken, its massive report was published in 1942, and so some of its impact was blunted by America's involvement in war. The study showed that students' success in college was unrelated to the studies they had followed in school. It was taken as a blow to the traditional disciplines-based curriculum, which universities insisted on as the only proper preparation for their academic programs. And it also supported the progressivist education movement — which funded the study — and its nontraditional integrated-curriculum programs, whose students did at least as well as students from traditional programs once in college.

The progressivist arguments had greater persuasiveness when only a small proportion of students went on to any kind of academic study. By 2010, however, a large proportion of the student population was seeking some kind of study after school years, and the colleges and universities were increasingly loudly complaining about the low standards of literacy and numeracy among the incoming students. The Salerno movement concentrated these complaints and emboldened scholars to take up the battle they had relinquished in the previous century for control over schools' curricula.

And a battle it became: a battle of words, of TV debates, of newspaper columns, of podcasts, of books. For the first time in a century, education and the curriculum became topics garnering significant media attention. Unfortunately, perhaps, this was a kind of attention that focused more on polemics and personalities than on the philosophical arguments. Initially, at least, it seemed a step up on the tired and boring arguments rehearsed endlessly between the old progressivists and traditionalists, until it became clear that those old arguments were in fact undergirding the new polemics.

"Salernoists," as they became called, planned an invasion of school boards and parent organizations, and sometimes there were unpleasant confrontations between them and teachers and teachers' organizations. Even more keenly, Salernoists clashed with organizations representing school administrators. These clashes did cause some rethinking of the role of schools and their relationship to knowledge and understanding. The trouble with the Salerno movement as a whole, especially as it grew rapidly in North America and Europe and spread to most countries with developed education systems, was that too few of its members had thought or read much about education, so for the most part they just loudly repeated old traditionalist positions.

Now we need to step back a bit from the dramatic conflict between the academic community in general and the school and its agents. The slogan that the school was the most anti-intellectual institution in society was clearly absurd at one level, but the slur hurt because of the apparent acceptance by so many progressivist educators, particularly at the elementary level of schooling, that the content of the curriculum was not very significant. The school had become a kind of therapeutic institution, focused more on trying to rescue children from so many social problems that capturing their imaginations with the wonder of mathematics and science had taken a decided second place. Added to that was the schools' buckling under to their political paymasters' demands for utilitarian work to improve test scores, some results of which were discussed earlier. The imagination wasn't recognized as contributing to paying any of those bills.

Given the choice of being student centered or knowledge centered, nearly all progressivist teachers knew where their commitment lay. Of course, they recognized that these two methods weren't mutually exclusive, and that knowledge was important, but the internalizing of the progressivist rhetoric always made teachers' organizations resist arguments such as those being pushed with new energy by the Salernoists.

Where was IE in this renewed polemical ferment? Odd alliances inadvertently helped IE have some small increases of visibility in regard to some general curriculum issues, and also one or two of its ideas began to be implemented here and there. One odd alliance might be described as being between Plato and the educational research measurement community.

One of Plato's ideas about education that made him the epitome of the worst feature of traditionalism, at least in the view of progressivists, was his notion that there were three different kinds of people — gold, silver, and bronze. The gold people were really smart and merited the efforts of educating, and the other two were not really thought about as educable in any serious sense. In part, this idea was so obnoxious to progressivists because they were largely committed to the social ideals of democracy, which in turn were associated with ideals of social equality and social equity. The writings of the socialist John Dewey helped to fix these associations as central to educational progressivists' beliefs.

An inconvenience with regard to this belief was the evidence from all kinds of testing that some children learned better than others whatever you did. One of the Salernoists' more effective attacks on professional educators was to point out that they employed the rhetoric of equality but ran a school system that fit exactly with Plato's ideas. It's just that contemporary educators were mealy-mouthed about the fact that their system divided children into classes, preparing some for advanced academic work, some for technical or skilled work, and the rest for nothing much. The Salernoists hit a nerve by accusing educators of massive hypocrisy, using rhetoric to disguise from themselves that they were sustaining a Platonic class system.

Gardner's popular multiple-intelligences theory received a serious sideswipe from this Salernoist argument. The Salernoists claimed that the theory's popularity was due largely to its hidden ideological attraction to those who wanted to disguise inequalities in achievement and assert equality wherever possible. So they argued that the multiple-intelligences theory had become a mainstream part of progressivism because it allowed educators to claim that everyone was intelligent, but in different ways. Whatever the actual empirical virtues of the theory as an explanation of different forms of human intelligence, which were considerable, and no matter that the claim about equality of intelligence nowhere appears in the theory itself, the assertion that it was educationally popular only for ideological reasons brought it into the center of the battle.

These were the kinds of polemics that were reported in the media. It was a messy polemic in that the educators were always able to turn around and claim to be doing only what their paymasters — in the end, the electorate — required of them.

IE also benefited from a confusion with traditionalist ideas, and this confusion affected its impact on the curriculum. To the embarrassment of many of those involved in IE, it became taken up by some of the more outspoken members of the Salerno movement. IE, it was clear to them, offered an approach to curriculum that was quite at odds with progressivist ideas. In particular, the IE insistence that a great deal of knowledge must be learned in order to stimulate the imagination appealed strongly to Salernoists; at least, the "great deal of knowledge" part appealed, and they saw the imagination stuff as harmless at worst. This alliance was based on the Salernoists' applying the principle that my enemy's enemy must be my friend. Proponents of IE were distinctly uncomfortable about this and tried to point out the difference between the traditionalist advocacy of certain privileged forms of knowledge or disciplines, and the IE belief that certain forms of knowledge and disciplines were important because they stimulated the development of appropriate cognitive tools and people's understanding.

Two curriculum changes began to make some headway as a result of the spread of IE ideas and practices. The first came in schools that had been among the earlier adapters of the ideas. After just a couple of years, seemingly spontaneously — except that it had been found to occur in all schools where a few teachers had been working with IE — teachers began to plan larger and larger units of study. That is, their overall "story" would often run for a semester, or even a year, and all the material they were mandated to cover within the curriculum became encompassed by the overarching story line. Relatedly, in such schools two and three and four or more teachers worked together to generate a single powerful story that would incorporate all that they had to teach for a year. So a group of teachers might decide that in their region, an important topic might be the lives of the aboriginal people, or farming practices, or the sheep trade, or the 1920s, or immigration. The whole curriculum then was related to this topic, ensuring that the required math, science, history, and so on, were incorporated to add to some dimension of the topic being explored over the semester or year.

One of the curriculum recommendations of IE was that every student should learn something in great depth, because the imagination could work only with knowledge the student had learned (and could do nothing with all the knowledge students had "learned how to learn" but never actually learned). A number of IE schools by mid-decade had begun to adopt the idea of arbitrarily allotting to each student in their first year of schooling a topic which they would study for the rest of their schooling. So one child might be given the topic of trains, another the Solar System, another mollusks, another food production, another teeth, and so on. Every month during their life at school they would work on their portfolio with a teacher. By the time they graduated from school, each student was well informed about something, and many, as it turned out, went on to study their topic in greater detail in universities. The fruits of this curriculum innovation in IE schools began to become apparent even early in the next decade, and it began to spread quite quickly. Graduates of those schools knew something in as much depth and breadth as almost anyone on earth. Such studies had a profound impact on their understanding of the nature of knowledge in general, which in turn impacted their understanding of the nature of everything else they learned.

The School: 2010–2020

Treating the curriculum and the school as distinct categories is far from ideal, as changes to one can be seen as changes to the other. But the school of 2020 would have been recognized immediately by anyone from the previous century. The greatest differences a visitor from the twentieth century would have noticed would have been in the students' clothes, and the teachers', and he or she might have been puzzled by some new pieces of technology, but mostly a walk round a school would have been readily familiar, and the technology would be quickly recognized as performing old tasks in only a slightly different way. But the school, too, was beginning to feel deep rumbles of change, not yet entering the front door of school buildings but harbingers of something that soon would become apparent.

In 2020, a second conference was organized by the Swedish woman responsible for the Salerno conference. This second conference was held in Vienna for symbolic reasons. It attracted 15,000 of the world's leading scholars, artists, writers, and scientists. There was unprecedented security on hand for an academic gathering. The aim of the conference was to produce a report about education, which came to be known as the Vienna Manifesto. It was about 35,000 words, was published in more than fifty languages, and within five years became one of the most widely read educational texts in history.

The Manifesto began with a historical introduction describing the cultural struggles that had occurred since the development of mass schooling. It characterized, a little too romantically some felt, the late nineteenth and early twentieth centuries as the time of one of the great cultural flowerings of human history. One of the greatest centers of that flowering was Vienna. The terrible mechanized slaughter of the Great War was a stun to that cultural development, followed by the rise of the killing ideologies that blighted human experience in the twentieth century and the massive destructiveness of World War II. The cultural flowering had disturbed almost all the old assumptions of the premodern world, and so had been feared and hated by many.

The Manifesto reached back to the German nineteenth century and brought into prominence again, with a new meaning and new combatants, the idea that what had been most at stake during the twentieth century had been the subject of a continuing *Kulturkampf,* or a Battle of Cultures, in the English version. The battle was described as being between a popular culture carried through ubiquitous electronic media that led to an impoverishment of the life of the mind and a culture built from the widest array of intellectual products produced in human history. The opening quotation of the Manifesto was taken from T. S. Eliot's *Notes Towards the Definition of Culture:* "In our headlong rush to educate everybody, we are lowering our standards, and more and more abandoning the study of those subjects by which the essentials of our culture . . . are transmitted; destroying our ancient edifices to make ready the ground upon which the barbarian nomads of the future will encamp in their mechanised caravans."

To many, this new Kulturkampf seemed like the old battle between elitist and popular cultures. This was explicitly accepted in the Vienna Manifesto, and it was represented, a little like the Salerno movement, as returning to a battle from which proponents of the older culture had retreated. The foundation of the public school had been seen by many as an opportunity to make the best education and cultural life available to all children. But that ideal was an early casualty of the drive to socialize and prepare the children of the working classes for the jobs the new industrial societies required. The Vienna Manifesto was a reassertion of the ideal that all children should be given access to a richer cultural inheritance than the school was providing. "Our children are being cheated out of their inheritance!" became another slogan taken from the Manifesto's pages.

An unfortunate simplification that occurred during the conference resulted from someone's suggesting that the Kulturkampf could be seen as pitting American popular culture against European bourgeois culture. Some prominent delegates derided the ethnocentrism of this characterization, but it was the one most commonly used, especially when the powerful and respected group of Nobel laureates from India, supported by Chinese scientists, used it. Simplistic and false though this crude representation of the Kulturkampf was, it gave definition to the struggles to follow.

Initially, following the dictum that those who are ignorant of history are condemned to repeat its mistakes, proponents of the Manifesto couched the conflict as being between such things as the supposed "universal" value of such "classics" as Beethoven's late string quartets compared with the wildly popular HooYa music nearly all young people were playing at the time.

Again, IE gained some additional visibility as a result of confusion. Once the tired old arguments were repeated and shown to be the same as ones that had been trotted out for more than a century, the IE language of "cultural tools" and "cognitive tools" was assumed to allow the same argument to be made in a different form. So, it was claimed, Beethoven's music was a cultural supertool, and when internalized, provided for each person a cognitive supertool that enlarged and enhanced understanding, sensibility, and so on. It was the old argument in new clothing, but the common use of the newer terms and the publicity it gave to IE gained IE ideas more influence.

Another term used frequently in the Manifesto — betrayal — was taken from a book first published in France in 1927, entitled *La trahison des clercs* (*The Treason of the Intellectuals*), written by Julien Benda. The Manifesto claimed that the betrayal of the energetic flowering of culture early in the twentieth century — not only in Europe, of course — had caused the greatest damage to modern cultural life. This betrayal was represented as one of the causes of the access to power of Hitler, Stalin, Mao Tse-tong, Pol Pot, and the other murderous despots who helped undo the intellectual and cultural promise with which the twentieth century began.

The Manifesto included, excessively, many felt, such words as "corruption," "degradation," "simplification," and so on, in describing what had been happening to the culture they valued, but basically it declared that the intellectuals would no longer betray culture but would engage in a Kulturkampf on behalf of a form of cultural life that they saw as liberating to the human spirit, and the Manifesto concluded that the first battleground was chosen: the school.

Conclusion

The ideological battles fought out during this decade, and the ecological crises that began to engulf societies during the following decades, tended to push into the background one of the persisting problems that sapped the energy of many teachers daily. That problem, or associated set of problems, was poverty, along with the gross disparity in wealth and the disparity in access to resources and power and to education in all contemporary societies. In some societies it was worse than in others, but in this decade the gap between rich and poor, on almost every scale, grew greater. From the educator's point of view, even when more liberal governments supplied significantly increased funding to the schools in poor areas, the job of educating was almost entirely hopeless. Broken families, impoverished conditions which did little to encourage the most basic self-discipline, easy access to drugs and the most debased forms of cultural life, hostility to school and what it stood for, and on through the litany of attitudes and experiences that made any achievement beyond the most basic literacy and numeracy almost insuperably difficult — and those most basic skills hard enough and not achieved by significant numbers of students. Routine tests of knowledge about the world given to school leavers exposed, in poorer students in particular, ignorance to a degree that stunned social commentators, politicians, and the more educated classes. The tests were very simple and asked only for the most rudimentary familiarity with topics that had been explicitly taught in the curriculum.

Many saw these results only as evidence of a waste of resources. Others, more alert to the catastrophic impoverishment of experience that such results exposed, saw these results as a massive condemnation of the hypocritical claims of democratic societies to offer "equality of opportunity" to all. Even the most purblind could not claim that children attending schools in slum areas had equal opportunities. As we shall see, the failure of the educational establishment to properly recognize the massive scale of injustice it was complicit in, and its failure to adequately respond to it, became a key reason for the transformation of schooling.

five

2020-2030

Education in the 2020s was greatly affected by the ecological crises of the decade. Warning voices had been loud for more than half a century, and it had finally become clear that the impact on advanced societies in particular was no longer ignorable. The cost of the massive programs of responses to the catastrophes was enormous. There were also huge anxieties that the draconian measures required to repair some of the immediately threatening environmental damage would turn out to be too little too late.

The economic and social disruption eventually brought the schools into crisis. There were what seemed at the time crises enough, as funding was increasingly diverted from schools to deal with more urgent priorities. The initiatives the schools took to play their part in responding to the environmental crises were the only projects for which funding was provided. Governments, when they took time off from managing the crisis and trying to address the various forms of environmental damage, mandated that all schools introduce new "ecological curricula," to ensure that children were equipped to understand the crises they faced, and to encourage behaviors that would mitigate the damage. One of the best-selling e-books of the time, written by a father and son and widely read in schools, was called *How Kids Can Help the Environment.*

The school was seen by many to be a crucial agent in responding to the ecological crises. For a long time, the school had not been generally applauded as a successful agency. Indeed, surveys continued to indicate that the population at large felt that schools were not performing their role well. Administrators within the school systems tended to shrug off such results; they had been hearing the same message for fifty years and more. As it was unclear just what the role of the school was supposed to be — the population of all modern states perceived it as having a number of different roles — administrators had never been sure how to respond adequately to the imprecise dissatisfaction represented in such surveys.

So mounting a powerful response to the ecological crises seemed to many within the school system as one clear route to renewing its popular appeal and again showing the relevance of the school to social problems. Progressivists in particular claimed that this engagement with the social problems of the time would make the school and curriculum more relevant to students' actual lives and problems. They harkened back to the early twentieth century, when the schools were an applauded social agency, helping to transform a mass of European peasants' children into well-socialized Americans within a decade of schooling.

More-cynical voices suggested that the streets did more than the schools to assimilate those immigrants into American life, and the wholesale mobilizing of the school to address the ecological crises was likely to be equally gratuitous. The school just isn't a good institution for such tasks, it was argued. It was the cynical view that was better supported by future events.

But these arguments were themselves fruitless, as other forces, like fear and the demands of their political paymasters, drove school administrators' decisions. Politicians and school administrators had to be seen doing something relevant to address the crises. These were anxious times, and too many didn't take the luxury of stopping to think whether the actions being proposed actually would have any effect on the problems or not. So the schools took on the ecological crises, and over the next decade or so brought upon themselves the conditions that would lead to significant and wholly unanticipated changes.

Teaching: 2020–2030

During this decade the IE modules for use in teacher education programs were used in increasing numbers of institutions. By the end of the decade, the two-week introductory module was being used with varying degrees of effectiveness in as many as a quarter of the programs in Europe and North America. It was seen as a useful option, and its distinctiveness made it attractive to instructors because they could feel that they were adding to their students' skill set. It also had the less-worthy virtue — and it is easy to underestimate the importance of this in the spread of IE — of having a series of terms, practices, techniques, and ideas that could become the subject of relatively clear assessment procedures. That is, it looked like knowledge and could be graded and so was attractive to instructors who liked easily "teachable" topics.

But success is hard to discount, and it was clear that many regular classroom teachers were having success with IE techniques. Not just success in exam results but also, and perhaps more important for its popularity among teachers, success in terms of their own job satisfaction: many teachers declared that they felt energized using IE procedures, and also that their students' were clearly more engaged and interested in learning. In the context of the general malaise that had settled on so many schools, this was widely noted by administrators. There was also a growing network of teacher support-groups for those committed to the IE approach. Universities taught IE M.Ed. programs, and workshops were available at many teachers' professional development days. There were also demonstration videos available, and many other forms of spreading knowledge and expertise in the use of IE.

But, despite all this, the proportion of students in classrooms exposed to IE forms of teaching remained quite small. It gained the reputation of a kind of "boutique" style of teaching, and most damagingly, gained the reputation of both being difficult to implement and also taking more preparation time. The claims of enthusiastic IE supporters, in articles, demonstration videos, in workshops, and so on, failed to make much impact against this reputation. Very many teachers just ignored it.

During the 2020s, then, IE enjoyed some evident successes in practice, but fewer than one-tenth of the students in the schools were ever exposed to any systematic IE experience. Even though increasing numbers of new teachers were being exposed to its methods, only a small proportion of those teachers became systematic users of it. Many of their instructors in colleges and universities were not themselves familiar with the background ideas, except in a superficial way, and it was becoming clearer to the groups promoting IE that a two-week exposure, often indifferently conducted, was insufficient to really engage more than a small proportion of student teachers in exploring the ideas and practices further. This was hardly a failure, of course, in that the decade did see a slow but gradual increase in its everyday use in schools. There were also a number of refinements in the planning frameworks, which made them easier for teachers to use. Despite it reputation for difficulty, it was becoming increasingly "user-friendly."

The Curriculum: 2020–2030

The history of the impact of IE on the curriculum during the 2020s can be broken into two parts. First, how IE fared as a result of the progressivist-led dedication of the school to helping the fight against the ecological crises, and second, how IE curriculum reforms began to go forward despite the overall shift in public schools' renewed sense of their important social role.

In the crisis-driven enthusiasm for "ecologizing the school," the Salernoists and their traditionalist allies received an unexpectedly sudden setback. Their agendas began to seem trivial in the face of the social dislocations and economic damage caused by the need to respond to the ecological crises. For populations under great pressure to adapt their economies and living conditions, the Salernoist proposals were branded an "ornament" that people could no longer afford. It was largely in vain that the Salernoists responded that only if students received the kind of academic education they proposed would the students become adequately equipped to respond to the current and likely future crises. Those with some historical perspective on public schooling saw this victory for progressivism as a replay of what had happened in the late nineteenth century in North America.

From its earliest years, IE had been closely associated with the development of an ecological consciousness. Many of its early adherents had urged educational preparation for the crises that had been predicted, and which by the mid-2020s were harrying the countries of the developed world. So, again for inadequate reasons, many school administrators began to turn to IE. It not only had a developed theory about ecological education but it also had many practical unit plans that had been implemented and refined over a number of years.

Wide-scale use of these units in the latter part of the decade contributed further to increasing educators' familiarity with IE, but their use, commonly without adequate training by the teachers on whom school administrators foisted them, was often superficial and dull. This was the first use of IE materials by many teachers who had little or no knowledge about the approach, and their very varied results did little to enhance IE's reputation among those who were encountering it for the first time.

More important for the future of IE's curriculum ideas was how it began to shape the curriculum in the few hundred schools that identified themselves as IE institutions. It might be easiest to show the kinds of changes that were occurring by following two students, rather rapidly, through a few days of their schooling. In 2028 Joe was a seven-year-old boy in Calgary and Bal a thirteen-year-old girl in Barcelona. Here we will be looking at the curriculum in IE schools of the time and largely ignoring the massive changes with regard to ecological training that were going on in the regular state-schools. Not that IE schools were free of the requirements for "eco-education," as it came to be known, nor did they want to be, but the changes in the IE curricula eventually had a more far-reaching impact than the changes to the state-school curricula.

Joe's Days

This segment is taken from a diary kept by a precocious seven-year-old. His language was unusually articulate, but even so it has been transliterated into a form easier to read, according to current practice.

Monday morning. Sunny. I walked to school with the chip on which I'd put the new things I'd learned for my portfolio on "dust." I've been "working on dust" — my dad says that as a joke — for two and a half years. Every week I've done some research. Because it rained yesterday, I didn't go to the track, so I was able to find out more for my new file on "dust that can explode."

Dust is solid particles with a diameter of less than 500 micrometers. That was the first entry. But my definition now runs to nearly a page (at first I spoke and the computer transcribed it, but now I write nearly all the entries). Yesterday I found this really neat stuff about the conditions in which certain forms of dust can explode. You need the moisture content of the dust to be over 11% and the oxygen content to be less than 12%. Ignition can be triggered if the temperature reaches more than about 410°. (I'm not exactly sure what all these terms mean, though I've got a vague sense, but I can ask Ms. Dutton, my portfolio supervisor, on Wednesday.) Dust is really interesting, and I reckon that in a few years, I'll know more about dust than almost anyone in the world. My best friend, Mick, has "leaves" as his topic. We're going to do a joint report at the end-of-year presentations about dust on leaves.

I may perhaps note here that this simple curriculum idea — that each child should study some arbitrarily assigned topic from the beginning to the end of his or her schooling — which was a staple of IE programs, was responsible for bringing additional attention to the approach during this decade. One oddity of this is that both traditionalists and progressivists agreed that the curriculum should provide both breadth and depth of knowledge, that is, all students should learn about the world and experience broadly, but they should also learn some things in detail. Traditionalists in particular had emphasized that close familiarity with some area of knowledge was necessary, if only so that students could understand that superficial acquaintance with a topic was often very misleading — they often quoted Alexander Pope's observation that "a little learning is a dangerous thing." Yet this principle never led them to invent anything like the simple innovation that became one distinctive mark of IE schools. This curriculum innovation brought together a number of principles: that the imagination worked best when it had access to a great deal of knowledge; that education required deep and extensive knowledge of at least something in particular; and that students during these years of their lives were strongly driven to collect knowledge as a kind of defense against the insecurity of an unknowably complex world. Many articles appeared in various media about IE's "young specialists." The obvious enthusiasm of nearly all children for their topics after a few years of detailed study was a signal educational success, and it was taken up by many schools who had no other connection with IE. It served as a kind of Trojan horse for IE. Back to Joe's diary.

In the classroom I slid back the desktop to check my schedule on the screen, to see where the rehearsal was for the freedom/slavery performance. Here's the world history curriculum we've been doing. In our first year, the curriculum focused on the great story of the universe around us and how the earth formed and how human beings came to spread around the planet and form the cultural groups and countries of today. While learning this story we also learned to read and write, to do some math connected with the story, and we began to study the other animals and plants and the great oceans that used to teem with life.

In our second year we studied the history of human beings again as a struggle for security against danger, from the earliest societies to the present. We learned about the many different kinds of dangers human societies had struggled against: the great cats and poisonous and destructive insects, and the bugs they caught from the animals they began to herd 10,000 years ago, and the dangers from each other — mainly from each other. We learned how as humans became more secure and began to grow in numbers, different groups competed for food and other resources and very readily fought battles and wars. Each episode of the story was brought out dramatically, and we played roles in acting them out. My favorite was the role I played in a raid on a medieval castle. We were shown how the technology of castle building seemed to give security, but this was undone by the increasingly clever technologies of digging under and smashing down castles.

And in this year we've been looking again at the story of human beings, but this year the focus is on the struggle for freedom against oppression. (Next year, we're going to see human history as the story of the struggle for knowledge against ignorance — one that Mr. Madoc says we aren't winning.) Today I had to play out my role as a Quaker man in 1855 who was helping slaves travel along the Underground Railway from the plantations they worked in Alabama to freedom in Canada.

During this year we have learned geography as it relates to the stories we have studied. We spent some of last week looking at maps of the U.S. and Canada and traced the "freedom roads" the slaves followed, as far as anyone now knows them. We had to get some adult to show us the Big Dipper and the pole star at night, and we had to imagine how important it was to the slaves heading north.

In the hall we had the three classes together. First Mr. Goshen had us spend a quarter of an hour singing the songs we've been learning. We started with "Go Down, Moses" and then "The Drinking Gourd." We were given the words to learn by heart. Each week we have to learn something by heart — Mother Goose rhymes, poems, parts of speeches. I've got quite a store of stuff I like to sing or just play over in my head now.

Tuesday. Began with Joke class. Rosario had been practicing at home to tell one of the question and answer jokes. He asked us:

"What do you get when you cross a snowman with a shark?"

No one guessed it.

"Frostbite!"

There was some laughter and brief applause for this. Then we discussed it, but there wasn't much to say about it, as we've told many jokes of this kind. I prefer the longer ones more. But Frank also had a question one: "What is a volcano?" "A mountain with hiccups." Some people liked that a lot, but I thought the hiccups aren't much like a volcano going off.

Sadie told a longer joke.

"Two women are arguing about whose dog is smarter. The first woman says, 'My dog is so smart that every morning he waits outside for the newspaper, takes it in his mouth, and brings it to me.'

"The second woman says, 'I know.'

" 'How do you know that?'

" 'My dog told me.' "

We half got the joke, but it was a problem till Sadie told us about newspapers being delivered to houses. Nearly everyone now enjoyed the story jokes over the simple question-answer ones — though some of those were clever and funny enough to score well on the weekly joke score lists. The one voted best of the day was Shaheen's.

"One night, Tim was walking home when, all of a sudden, a thief jumped on him. Tim and the thief began to wrestle. They rolled about on the ground and Tim put up a tremendous fight. However, the thief managed to get the better of him and pinned him to the ground. The thief then went through Tim's pockets and searched him. All the thief could find on Tim was twenty-five cents. The thief was so surprised at this that he asked Tim why he had bothered to fight so hard for the twenty-five cents. 'Was that all you wanted?' Tim replied. 'I thought you were after the five hundred dollars I've got in my shoe!' "

Some kids in our class still have problems with jokes like that. In discussion a few said they thought Tim was silly to have confessed about the five hundred dollars, and they had to have it explained how that was what made it into a joke. It was — I'd learned the word last week with regard to a similar joke — the *incongruity* that made it funny.

Then, in the afternoon, we had a session in the computer room, six of us. Language study. We are learning to sing some of the sailors' songs from the time of the slave trade. " 'Blow, Boys, Blow" was the most popular, and "Aweigh, Santy Ano," and "Old Swansea Town Once More." This last was a windlass and capstan shanty — a song sung by sailors as they turned the capstan to lift the anchor. We are learning a lot of words and some sense of what it was like for sailors in the old days long ago.

For the last hour of the day, for our history study, we chose as a class to fill in some of the background of the opening up of the seas by the slave trade, and so we are studying pirates and hearing stories of the great pirates. This week we are learning about women pirates. I didn't know there were so many. We made a card and a file for each one of the most famous. In 1805 Ching Shih became the leader of the great Red Flag Fleet, a gang of pirates with over 1,500 ships. They sailed along the whole Chinese coast and south to Malaysia — we had to check out the maps again. Chinese officials tried all kinds of ways to bring the Red Flag Fleet to justice, but they always failed to defeat the pirates. The Chinese navy lost sixty-three ships in the attacks. Even the navies of Portugal and Britain could not defeat Ching Shih. Finding it hopeless trying to fight her, the government offered a general amnesty to all pirates in 1810 and Ching Shih decided to take advantage of it. She negotiated pardons for almost all of her men. She retired with her huge fortune, ran a gambling house, and had at least one son. Some historians say that she was the "best pirate who ever lived."

Each of us is keeping a list of people whose names we have come across who were at sea in those years or who owned ships. We started with the names, then divided them into merchants, slaves, naval officers, pirates. We are now breaking the lists down further and adding categories. After today's stories, I will break my pirates into a male and female set.

Bal's Blog

A blog by a fourteen-year-old student, Bal, in Barcelona describes a couple of days of her IE schooling and translates as follows. It had clearly been written to a friend of hers in another country, trying to describe her experience over a few days.

On Wednesday we began, as we do on Mondays and Fridays too, with our quarter-hour "People Past and Present" class. We have a regular schedule in which each of us, and the teacher, is responsible for researching and then making a presentation about a particular person. Usually people find someone heroic, though some kids go for real villains. We have a computer template that we can use — it has a place for a picture or video of the person, then places for text and verbal commentary. What we try to do is bring out the unusual qualities of the person, showing what makes her heroic in one way or another — the teacher uses the phrase "transcendent human qualities" all the time. In a short time, looking at someone's life or particular achievements, you can usually find something awesome or moving. We've had people from all times and places — there's no rule at all about who you can choose. A quarter of an hour isn't long, but some students haven't yet learned how not to be boring. We can ask questions, and sometimes you can get them to tell you the really interesting bits about someone, so the students tend to learn quite quickly how to "mine the heroic" as the teacher says.

This week we had Maria do one on the ancient Chinese jokester and philosopher, Chuang Tse. It included the scene when he was dying. His disciples asked him where he wanted to be buried. He said he'd rather just be taken out to some wasteland when he was dying so that he could see the stars and then just be left there. His disciples were horrified, and said:

"But Master, if we leave you out like that the birds will eat you."

"If you bury me, the worms will eat me. What have you got against birds?" He was an odd guy, very funny and profound as well. It was a great presentation.

Today, Andres presented on Shah Jahan, the Indian emperor who built the magnificent Taj Mahal as a memorial to his beloved wife. There were more images of the temple than of the emperor, and someone said they weren't sure who the hero really was: the building or the person. But the five-minute discussion led to Andres saying he would revise to show better how the temple grew out of Shah Jahan's love of his wife and passion for architecture. (Shah Jahan, he said, meant "king of the world." Bit optimistic.) On Friday, we have a presentation by Ramon about the American athlete Jesse Owens, then so far scheduled for next week are Hildegard of Bingen, Marie Curie, Oscar Wilde, the great Portuguese athlete of the past decade, Céu Roldão, and next Friday we have the Catalan all-round strange guy, Ramon Lull.

We then went to our monastery class, which lasts for two hours. One of the topics we have been studying this year — because you will see many old monasteries in our country — are what these buildings are, why they were built, and who occupied them, and what they are used for today, because only a very few are still inhabited by monks. We have been studying their history, and who first had the idea of monasteries. We discovered that communities of men dedicated to some spiritual ideals have been common in many cultures, even in the ancient world. We learned about who organized them, and who founded the tradition of monasteries we see in Western countries today. St. Benedict, who was a twin, and whose sister was the holy nun, St. Scholastica, wrote the first Rule for monasteries and founded the first Christian monasteries in Europe.

In these classes we study all the subjects you study in your school, but we do it as part of some general project. We'll be studying monasteries for a month. We'll look at their history and the people who were most influential in making monasteries work. We are also reading for literature class *The Chronicle of Jocelin of Brakelond*, about a monastery in England at Edmundsbury. I must say I was surprised to find that it's really interesting. It's about the daily life of a monastery in the Middle Ages. It was run by the wise, firm, yet gentle abbot Samson and describes all the daily goings-on and disputes among the monks. But what is really weird is how they didn't really think of their daily world as cut off from a supernatural world at all. You get a fascinating sense of a really different consciousness. And they had allotments of gallons of beer each week! We thought this meant they would be drunk all the time, till the teacher told us it was to help sterilize the water and was very weak.

But their business is also a part of our math study. They borrowed money, "one thousand and two score pounds," from William FitzIsabel for the running of the monastery, and four hundred pounds from Isaac, son of Rabbi Joce, and eight hundred and four score pounds from Benedict, the "Jew of Norwich." They also borrowed some smaller amounts from Benedict, such that after fourteen years they owed him one thousand two hundred pounds. We had to calculate the interest that was charged, and then study the document for information on how Abbot Samson raised the money year by year to pay off the debt before he died. I know, it sounds a bit weird, but it was fascinating delving into the actual lives of these old guys. We produced a cash flow chart of the monastery's finances over a twenty-year period beginning while Hugh was abbot and through the period of Samson being abbot. (My Portfolio, which we build from the beginning of our schooling to the final year, is on money, so I have been able to incorporate this into my portfolio. Always great to get two kicks at the same can.)

We prepared a set of People cards for each of the members of the monastery, beginning from Jocelyn's descriptions of the almoner, the sacristan, the cellerer, the dean, the prior, and so on. We also did a study of the chants the monks sang during the day, and practiced some of these in two groups across the class, like they did in the choir stalls. We also learned some of the popular songs of the time. In art work we incorporated some of the designs we found on old monasteries or in documents into our own cards and reports.

Our "Technology of Everyday Things" class, on Wednesday afternoons, is about the ergonomics of the utensils in the monastery and the furniture they built. In science we studied the instruments they devised to measure time, which also had to ring bells or make some noise to wake the monks up to sing in the choir or to go to services. We did a brief class on how that technology led, in the end, to space ships — the way one thing leads to another. We also have a class on Mondays and Fridays on Ideas, and we are studying the Rule of St. Benedict and discussing the idea of monasteries, and what stimulated them and sustained them for so long. We wondered whether there weren't some features of monastic life that might be good for us to try to bring into our lives.

So we have an intensive month-long look at monasteries, and will continue some of the work we began in our literature class, where we have some way to go in reading Jocelyn's chronicle. Everyone has also learned some Latin, and a few want to carry on with that in their optional classes. Ecological ideas are also furthered by studying the relationship of the monasteries to their environment. How did they deal with their waste, what results occurred from monasteries being the most innovative farmers in the whole Middle Ages period, and that kind of thing.

The blog ends here.

During that decade, while students in IE schools were being exposed to a varied curriculum, the general curriculum of the regular schools was changed significantly to serve the social cause of responding to the ecological crises.

The form of IE education had already moved to a much more flexible day with overarching stories or narratives giving purpose and meaning to the smaller curriculum areas within. This is not to say that IE schools remained uninterested in accommodating their curricula to the ecological crises. Rather they claimed that their curricula had been sensitive to ecological issues from the beginning and that they were preparing their students to be well equipped to respond to the crises.

The School: 2020–2030

Two main innovations in the regular school systems that were to have significant future repercussions came into play during the 2020s. The first — already mentioned — was the mobilizing of the school and its curriculum to help fight the ecological battles of the day. Many applauded this for making the schools and teaching "relevant" to the outside world, and for involving students in the world outside the school walls. Complex programs were set in place that arranged for students to visit frontline sites in the battles. These might be laboratories, for example, in which attempts were being made to help re-stock the oceans with various forms of life that had been largely destroyed by overfishing, which had led to the unexpectedly rapid and catastrophic collapse of the whole ocean life-cycle. Also visited were reforestation projects, experimental nonpolluting transportation stations, sites where the most dramatic effects of climate change were evident, and so on. Though efforts were made to continue the traditional academic programs, and to fit lessons in mathematics and science around ecological themes and so make them relevant to the ecological crises, the experience of nearly all children in school was mainly about learning the causes and potential cures for the damage that was affecting their lives. Much effort was spent on teaching them to be, as it was commonly put, a part of the solution and not part of the problem. By the end of the decade these programs were in full swing across the developed world.

Conclusion

IE entered this decade with growing visibility and an anomalous position within education. Educational arguments continued to be conducted in terms of the old bifurcation between the progressivists and traditionalists. In both groups there were "hard-nosed, common-sense" people who saw the purpose of schools as primarily to prepare the next generation of citizens with the right values, and the new workforce with the right skills — they saw the school as ideally a flexible institution, attuned to society's present and future needs and prepared to shift its agenda to fit those needs. IE ideas fared moderately well with all groups because its teaching ideas were widely accepted by the progressivists and its curriculum ideas were widely accepted by the traditionalists. As IE schools showed consistently good results on standardized tests, they also gained wide if vague general approval by those who used such tests as the proper measures of schooling success.

The growing number of schools — perhaps a couple of hundred by the middle of the decade — that identified themselves as specifically focused on IE attracted attention, however, because they were effective in engaging students and in achieving unusually successful results in literacy, numeracy, and science. As IE theory became better known during the 2020s it also became the target of increasing criticism, and disputes arose among IE proponents about how it should best be interpreted and implemented.

One continuing problem faced by the IE movement was due to the apparently unshakable assumption by many that anything concerned with the imagination had to be connected with "the arts." Despite the many books and articles and conferences and seminars in which the main proponents of IE asserted again and again that the ideas were about engaging the imagination in science and mathematics no less than in the arts, the assumption persisted among many that it was a form of education dedicated primarily to the arts. As with most confusions, this had some beneficial as well as unfortunate effects for IE. One of the unfortunate effects was the slowness with which "mainstream" curriculum specialists began to attend to IE's potential contribution to math and science teaching and curricula. The beneficial effects tended to be connected to the enthusiasm for and the imaginative application of the ideas in various arts programs. The slight irony of this early enthusiasm for the approach in the fine arts, voiced frequently by proponents of IE, was that teachers of the arts needed it least. It was the science and math teachers who needed it more.

But despite theoretical disputes, there was a growing recognition that students who had been exposed to IE for much of their schooling simply looked like educated people to pretty well all educational factions. That is, they tended to be widely knowledgeable and enthusiastic about some area of knowledge in detail. Nearly all had developed musical interests, and most played some instrument. They were scientifically literate and read widely in fiction as well as other areas. It would be easy to exaggerate this difference from other students who had experienced a more regular schooling, but it was commonly recognized when the students entered universities. Professors began to accept as an adequate explanation of some students' good work and attitudes to learning that they had come from an IE school. Certainly many other students received excellent teaching, but students from IE backgrounds seemed to exemplify educational virtues more routinely.

I have mentioned that ecological crises played an important role in bringing about significant changes to the school, and I will discuss it further in the following chapter. But I should also mention that even without the crises, most historians of this period agree that something similar would have happened. That is, the schools in most advanced nations — increasingly unsuccessful at producing students with academic skills at a sufficiently high level, and continuingly unsuccessful at significantly introducing the "bottom half" of the schools' population to the tools for understanding available from their cultural history — still justified themselves in terms of social and personal fulfillment criteria. Few educational writers at the time argued that the growing emphasis on the socialization functions of schooling would lead to the kinds of academic inadequacies that in fact occurred. That is, the ecological crises were merely the particular events that brought to a head the situation the school was inevitably moving toward, given the set of ideas which guided educational decision making at the time.

The global social and economic disruptions of the 2030s continued to cause major distress, especially among First World societies. By the end of the tumultuous decade, however, there were signs of hope that the worst predicted impacts of the ecological crises might be avoided. The costs were vast, but almost any cost seemed worthwhile for those glimmers of hope. But they were only glimmers, and anxieties persisted that the first signs of effective responses to the crises might yet be overwhelmed.

As some sense of stabilization and control was beginning to be felt with regard to the environment, the turmoil over the school was increasing. The radical restructuring that was tried in some districts toward the end of the 2030s can be seen as the beginning of trends that gathered force during the 2040s. So what is described here is just the start of the greatest change that overcame the schools since their founding in the mid- and late nineteenth century.

In short, the commitment of so many school resources to the social and environmental crises came under aggressive attack on three grounds, each given strength by the slight easing of the ecological crises. First, and perhaps predictably, the Salernoists and their Vienna Manifesto allies argued that all the efforts spent on shifting the schools' curricula to make them "relevant" to the crises had been in fact irrelevant to the programs that demonstrated some success in impacting the crises, and the costs in terms of general education had been enormous. "We might have ecologically alert students," claimed Dr. Amato, head of the Salernoists through most of the decade, "but we also have students who are scoring less well on all tests of general knowledge and understanding, and especially they are sliding further in scores on science, math, and literacy." It was, perhaps also predictably, people highly skilled in those areas of knowledge that were able to generate imaginative and effective responses to the ecological problems. Ideological awareness was bought at the cost of the knowledge and skills that might actually have been useful, it was claimed.

Second, the incautiousness of the schools' commitment to social concerns had produced, some argued, a generation of ecoterrorists, or as some called them, referring back to an earlier mass mobilization of a youthful population, ecological Red Guards — that is, many students were imbued with a righteousness concerning their own ecological behavior. The encouragement they had received in schools from zealous teachers led to gangs of students branding specific behavior by individuals, businesses, and other social agents and agencies as damaging to the environment, and, to use their term, "eco-bad."

Third, the public and politicians who had earlier demanded schools do something radical to address the crises now turned on the schools for the inadequacy of the programs and changes they had put in place. Given ammunition from extensive studies sponsored by the Salernoists, who had rapidly regained the influence they had lost during the worst of the crises, the public and politicians also renewed their attacks on the school systems' further reduced effectiveness in teaching literacy, science, and mathematics. The "skills/knowledge crisis," as it was dubbed, became a major focus of media attention. This led to recognition that the schools' role in socializing students, or "ideologizing" them, as the Salernoists called it, had interfered with the academic role of the school. And this in turn led to various experiments with the organization of schools during the decade.

Employees of the public education systems were distressed and somewhat bewildered by the rapid decline in public support for the schools and began to feel a new vulnerability. For a century and a half it had been taken for granted that there would be occasional bouts of public disaffection with schools but that careful accommodation to the causes of complaint would gradually subdue them: if there were complaints about programs being too academic, then more "relevant" programs were developed; if there were complaints about lack of preparedness for the workplace, then greater emphasis was put on vocational training; when basic academic skill levels declined, programs to boost scores in those areas were introduced — though the continuing inadequacy of such programs was the cause of abrasive complaints. Proponents of these programs continued to argue, with the support of teachers' groups, that their apparent ineffectiveness was due to the fact that they hadn't been put into practice properly because of competing demands placed on schools, demands made by the very people who were now complaining.

But it had never entered anyone's mind that the school itself might face radical restructuring in response to widespread disapproval by the society the schools were supposed to be serving. The Salernoist term "a failing institution" began to gain wide currency. It was a decade in which teachers' anxiety levels were consistently high.

Teaching: 2030–2040

It would be fair to say that the teaching profession as a whole was in something close to turmoil for much of the decade. "Turmoil" in a profession, of course, doesn't capture well what any particular teacher does in any particular school day by day. Entering any school during the decade would not provide easy evidence of turmoil, as teachers went about their familiar tasks in classrooms with groups of twenty to thirty students each organized by age. But the word does capture something of the intensity of initiatives that were supposed to address the problems of the "failing institution." Teachers were subjected to what seemed to be a ceaseless barrage of inquisition, testing, and curriculum initiatives to be implemented. The resulting stress was cited by many teachers as their reason for leaving the profession. New teachers were recruited, and, inevitably, the standards of academic achievement required for an increasingly disrespected profession declined.

Educational thinking, in general, remained a captive of the few ideas that had dominated it for so long. Progressivists asserted that more child-centered programs were required, that students' interests should determine the curriculum, that more attention should be given to research that exposed the nature of children's development and learning styles, and that teaching must conform with the findings of this research, and so on. The apparent lack of success of this package of ideas and practices in the past was put down to its not having been implemented adequately. More teacher education and more workshops were demanded. And money was provided for these programs by nervous political authorities. But money was also provided for Salernoist alternatives, and these led to rigorous implementations of traditional ideas, even more systematically applied.

Within each of these broad schools there were many variants, so often a single school district had radically different programs enacted in neighboring schools. In some degree this had always been the case since mass schooling began, but the starkly different experiences students went through during this decade, all labeled "education," began to undermine even further the public perception that those running the schools really had any clear conception of what they were supposed to do to educate people.

It was during this decade, however, that IE made its most significant gains. To some degree it had long been hindered by some of its distinctive features having been co-opted by its progressivist and traditionalist competitors. One significant condition for its quick growth in the 2030s was the recognition of its distinctness from educational philosophies that were coming increasingly into disrepute.

The crucial event for many was a debate at the 2033 meeting of the Americas' Educational Research Association meeting in Vancouver, Canada. As this city had been associated with the beginning of IE, it was felt appropriate to hold, as a central session in the largest convention hall, two debates: one between a representative of IE and a leading progressivist, and another the following day between a representative of IE and a leading Salernoist. This event was somewhat serendipitous, and probably no one would have suggested it had the conference not been held in Vancouver. Someone during the planning sessions had the idea of featuring something connected with the host city, and someone else remembered that IE was based there. The event itself wasn't hugely dramatic, indeed some felt the debates were rather dull, but the fact that IE was given so prominent a place elevated significantly many educationalists' sense of its importance.

Accessible through the Internet and seen by administrators and policy makers around the world, the debates marked the beginning of widespread adoption of IE ideas and practices, though it took more than a decade for the programs to become generally implemented. To a significant degree, IE's success was probably seen as the failure of the progressivist and traditionalist alternatives. At a time of vigorous disputes and questioning of schooling, IE seemed to offer a fresh alternative, even though many who supported its adoption were not at all clear about its underlying foundations. Some people just liked its practices and its general success, and others liked its insistence on students' mastering of a wide array of knowledge. Because it had an appeal, brought out in the debates, to both those with residual sympathies for progressivism and those favoring traditionalism, it proved relatively easy to get widespread agreement among people who had earlier been in conflict about educational policy.

The debates were unfair in that they gave a clear advantage to the IE representatives, Preet Basi and Gordon Flyte. That is, both the progressivist, Marian Banerjee, and the Salernoist, Owen Gwynek, were put on the defensive to begin with because they felt the pressure of public blame for the schools' failing society in some ill-defined, and variously defined, ways. Their presentations were largely attempts to divert blame, whereas the IE presentations could sound an upbeat and positive note, proclaiming new ideas, new practices, and parading successful results. Drs. Basi and Banerjee debated on the Wednesday of the conference and Drs. Flyte and Gwynek on the following day.

The IE representatives both began by explicitly tying their opponents' ideas to the perceived failures of the schools. This debating strategy worked to the IE advantage because the progressivist and traditionalist programs, after all, were still those most prominent in the schools, and though the IE methods of teaching were increasingly widely used, they bore none of the general criticism sustained by the educational establishment. The progressivist and traditionalist champions were also at a disadvantage because Drs. Basi and Flyte were arguing on behalf of a program whose distinctiveness they were keen to emphasize, whereas Drs. Banerjee and Gwynek both began by suggesting that IE had much in common with their programs. Indeed, they both made the seriously bad move of taking a slightly patronizing tone in claiming IE was just a form or offshoot of their own programs. This allowed Drs. Basi and Flyte to further underline the differences with those increasingly discredited programs and to assert that any similarity their opponents saw was a product of their own confusion.

Banerjee and Basi, coincidentally born within a few miles of each other at close to the same time in Poona, India, had been given half of an hour each to sketch the central position of their programs, indicate why they believed those programs were best equipped to carry the schools toward a better future, and propose what had to be done for this better future to be brought into being. After the presentations, the speakers were invited to engage in a more informal debate based on their position statements. Drs. Banerjee and Basi stood at podiums at either side of the stage.

Here are some extracts from the exchanges that followed the opening presentations. The first set is from day 1 and the second from day 2.

BANERJEE: You have said, again and again, that your focus is on understanding the tools students have available for learning, and shaping teaching accordingly. This is no different from a central principle of progressivism since the beginning: understand the student's stage of development and style of learning and teach accordingly. As we have frequently said and demonstrated, we find many of the methods of teaching you have developed excellent, and we have encouraged our teachers to incorporate them into their own skill set.

BASI: But our teaching methods are tied to our underlying principles. You ignore an insight of one of your founding figures. John Dewey said that in education the end and the means are tied together. He wanted teachers to use discovery methods, for example, not because they were most efficient, but because they best mirrored the methods of scientific exploration, and it was that form of thinking that constituted his educational aim. That is, the aim of educating was tied up with the means. And so it is with IE. We build narrative structures into lessons, and use an array of other cognitive tools, because the aim of IE is to maximize for each child the flexible use of that array of cognitive tools available from cultural history.

BANERJEE: But we have no objection to that as an educational aim, which is why we can adopt the methods so straightforwardly. It's just that you use a different language.

BASI: But if you take seriously Dewey's principles, you will see that our aim of engaging the imagination in knowledge about the world . . .

BANERJEE: Which we also share. You mustn't think that we have no . . .

BASI: But you do not share with us the principle that these methods can be learned *only* in the context of the knowledge in which they exist in cultural history or in present use. That is, we require the students to learn a great deal of knowledge because only by seeing those "tools" at work in knowledge can their imaginations play with it and their understanding grow.

BANERJEE: There, too, we are not in disagreement, I believe, except about your claim that the students somehow need to store all this knowledge in their memories, as though the knowledge is something that needs to be stuffed in a mind-box. We have long pointed out that it is the procedures of learning that are important for the student to master. They do not also have to remember all that knowledge. The Internet and libraries are full of knowledge. What the student needs to know is how to access the knowledge needed at any particular time, and to know how to use it appropriately for their needs.

BASI: Well, at least you will have to concede that we disagree about this. We believe it is your focus on procedural knowledge rather than on content that has been a source of the persistent weakness of progressivism as an educational theory. Or rather, it is your consistent separation of the two that has been the cause of problems. Students' imaginations can only work with what they know. All the knowledge on the Internet is educationally useless to the development of students' imaginations if they only know how to "access" it but don't know it. I often think that your "child-centered" philosophy has led to a blindness about the role of knowledge in educating — which is why it is impossible to build any distinctively progressivist curriculum and why you are happy to say you share our educational aims, even though it is clear to us that you very obviously don't. The procedures, the methods, the tools are tied into the knowledge in which they have developed. You can't have them on the cheap — that is our central disagreement with progressivism: you want education on the cheap, without the work of learning and the pleasures of knowing.

BANERJEE: That, of course, is nonsense. We want students' own sense of inquiry to carry them into the world of knowledge. We share an end but differ in our means — that's all. It is your insistence on "work" that doesn't chime well with our sense of what the classroom should be like for children — a place of exploration, of pleasure, of openness. We do not differ about students' learning; it's just that we trust the child's own instincts more than you. We believe that greater freedom in the classroom opens up the possibility of greater learning. As I said in my opening statement, it is not progressivist ideas that are at fault, but rather it is the constraints on schools and teachers, and the incessant intrusive testing, that prevent the natural inclinations of the child to find adequate outlets. If we were allowed to organize schools according to our educational philosophy our successes would be evident to all. Though you keep insisting on your difference from progressivism, it is surely clear that IE classrooms put into practice similar principles and beliefs about students' learning. Your classrooms are dedicated to students' imaginative engagement in what they are learning — no differently from our progressivist classrooms.

BASI: But you can tell immediately if you are in a progressivist or an IE classroom — you would surely agree? The differences . . .

BANERJEE: I wouldn't agree for a moment. I have been in many IE classrooms and could easily have been in progressivist classrooms. I see the same concern for children's styles of learning and . . .

BASI: But your understanding of styles of learning is quite different from our concern with cognitive tools. The classrooms can look alike only if you are observing their most superficial features. Our focus is on what the students will have in common in the way of a working tool kit for understanding, whereas you are seeking all kinds of indicators of psychological difference and functioning and neurophysiological data of only the most marginal significance for educational practice . . .

This early exchange, which became sharper as time went on, really didn't resolve any issues. People in the audience felt that it was mainly a rehash of positions that never really came to grips with each other. Yet, oddly, over the next weeks and months it was taken as a clear victory for IE, especially as the next day's debate, felt to be similarly indecisive by those present, added to the sense of IE as a clearly distinct and new and more promising approach to educating.

Dr. Banerjee's insistence that IE was quite like progressivism became increasingly a problem for her through the discussion period that followed the debate in that it seemed as though she was willing to credit IE with all the strengths of progressivism, allowing it also to lay claim to the strongest point of the Salernoist/traditionalist program. From the preceding routine assertions of their positions, the only line that had a potent life in the polemical battles to come was Dr. Basi's much quoted: "You want education on the cheap, without the work of learning and the pleasures of knowing." Again, this was an unfair characterization, as Dr. Banerjee forcefully asserted, but rhetorically it had great influence, especially as it was prominently used in subsequent IE media news briefs.

On Thursday the debate between Drs. Flyte and Gwynek attracted another large crowd. The opening statements were unremarkable, though Flyte's had been carefully coordinated with Basi's of the previous day, and their combined effect was to give an attractive view of IE's distinctiveness. Only in the following discussion did contentious issues arise. Dr. Gwynek followed the same rhetorically unwise strategy that Dr. Banerjee had the previous day, beginning by insisting that the distinguishing feature of IE was really just another form of traditionalist practice.

GWYNEK: Yesterday your representative insisted on a strong distinction between IE and progressivism by emphasizing your commitment to students' mastery of curriculum material. You keep insisting that your ideas are distinct from ours, too, but it seems to me that it is only a difference of flavor rather than anything more profound. That is to say, we share the aim of producing a knowledgeable student, familiar with the canon of knowledge generated in cultural history. You talk about certain forms of knowledge generating or stimulating the development of understanding—you have cited certain very potent cultural materials, such as Shakespeare's plays or Darwin's theories or Chung Tse's parables, as "supertools" in students' educational development. Well, apart from the peculiar language, these are positions we have long held. The mind is made up of the knowledge it learns, and if we want good minds, we need to learn good things, and plenty of them. This, I think, is a view you also share?

FLYTE: I think the differences between IE and your conception of education are subtle but profound. You build a curriculum of certain canonical works, knowledge, art forms, and so on, because you believe that knowing them *is* education. We see them as valuable only because they are rich in the cognitive tools in whose development education lies. Now that looks the same to you, except we seem to be adding an unnecessary item, the "cognitive tools," which you are willing to overlook. But that "unnecessary item" is extremely important. We do not believe that education resides in mastery of a particular canon. It resides in mastery of cognitive tools. The canon you value can indeed be helpful in building the students' tool kit of understanding, but there are many ways, many diverse forms of knowledge, many different cultural routes to achieve the building of the tool kit.

GWYNEK: That begins to sound relativistic to me. I am not clear why you are so eager to dissociate yourself from a set of ideas you clearly agree with. I have here an IE curriculum [he waves a disc aloft]; in some ways it is more rigorously content-oriented than anything you will find in a traditionalist school. A good case . . .

FLYTE: But education isn't the curriculum. One of the statements used earlier in our movement, which has always struck me as too imprecise . . . but I'll quote it here because it seems apposite: "All knowledge is human knowledge; it grows out of human hopes, fears, and passions. Imaginative engagement with knowledge comes from learning in the context of the hopes, fears, and passions from which it has grown or in which it finds a living meaning." Well, the wording was something like that, and there's obviously a problem with the simplistic suggestion of causality in it. But what it gets at is the way knowledge, to us, grows in the mind and can engage the imagination; it is tied to emotions implicated in the knowledge and tools . . .

GWYNEK: But I have no disagreement with your quotation. We do not believe that the curriculum is education. We acknowledge that it must be brought to life in the classroom. We know that the most knowledgeable person is not the best educated; the knowledge has to be learned along with a range of human qualities that can allow the knowledge to be put to good work. You are presenting only a travesty of the traditionalist program.

FLYTE: I'm sorry if so, but I am trying to emphasize a difference between our positions, which you seem reluctant to acknowledge or see as important. Dr. Banerjee yesterday gave an account of how progressivists see knowledge growing in the mind, and she referred a lot to neurophysiology and psychology. My concern with your Salernoist program is its apparent belief that familiarity with particular kinds of knowledge forms the basic building block of the educated mind, and I think that this leads to a fetishizing of particular curriculum content, leads to rigidity, and gives excessive credit to the relatively superficial intellectual ability needed to learn and recall this core curriculum of valued knowledge. Now, I confess, how knowledge grows in the mind in the process of education continues to mystify me a little, though of course IE does have its theories. But we offer a third way between the progressivist view and yours. In IE, the aim is the development of cognitive tools, and it is recognized that many forms of knowledge can contribute to this. The theory of IE, that is, gives both flexibility in, and a clear set of criteria for, the construction of the curriculum. By contrast the traditionalist curriculum is rigid and the progressivist curriculum is vague.

Well, the discussion continued. The phrase that was quoted by Dr. Flyte, about all knowledge being human knowledge and tied up with passions and fears — a phrase that Dr. Gwynek agreed with — was put to a lot of promotional work by IE. The agreement was lost, and the phrase was taken as a decisive difference between IE and traditionalist/Salernoist forms of education. It somehow convinced people that traditional forms of education lacked heart, and lacked a feeling for the human core of the enterprise. This was clearly unfair, but history, as Thucydides said, is neither fair nor predictable, except that it is predictable in its unpredictability.

After the debates many of the IE proponents picked up on the casual phrase Flyte had used about a "third way" of educating, encouraged by its frequent use in IE media briefings and infomercials. The "third way" was of course an ancient slogan, used by political parties, ideological movements, and religious subgroups for centuries. It had nearly always been an attractive way of implying that the two dominant, opposing groups might both have some valuable insights but also serious confusions, and a third group would carry forward the good ideas and leave the bad behind. Slogans are not used to make arguments but to capture something important about a movement to promote it in an advantageous way. That is, a slogan is not something to think deeply about, but it is useful because it distills an idea or feeling that people may be ready to be persuaded by. And something about the times meant that the educational world was ready for IE.

So the debates worked very much to IE's advantage. First, they elevated IE's visibility in the educational world. Second, both the IE spokespeople played the appealing role of the bright newcomer that had taken up the strong points of the old discredited movements. They also did a good job of presenting IE as an attractive new form of educating that had already accumulated some impressive results, indicating success in a wide variety of educational contexts. Little recognition was given to the significant disadvantages Drs. Banerjee and Gwynek were under, and subsequent complaints about the format made by both progressivists and Salernoists were passed off as "sour grapes" or, given the Salernoist movement's association with that region of Italy, "sour lemons."

Third, the central group of IE proponents followed up the debates with a clever media campaign that consistently highlighted the few passages mentioned above. It was in part responsible for the growing conviction that the ideas and practices of IE were decisively superior to the ideas and practices of its debate opponents. There was no very good reason to believe this, but the David and Goliath story played its usual role in the retelling of what the debates had established.

Fourth, the accumulation of these results seemed to offer to educational administrators a way out of the current troubles that beleaguered them. So, largely for political reasons — though many had been persuaded by the arguments presented during the debates and in IE literature — educational administrators started using the language of the new "third way." It presented them with a strategy for distancing themselves from the perceived failures of the school system in the past, and it allowed them to see themselves as offering a new approach and a new direction. And to a significant degree it worked for them. IE was recognized as new, and it did have a good track record in regular schools, and it was distinctive. Politicians were persuaded that a solution had been found to the schools' problems, and money was released for retraining teachers, for equipping schools with IE materials, for workshops for in-service teachers, and for the whole panoply of educational activities that had long been a part of the process of change.

The above may seem to be a rather long introduction to only a brief description of the changes that occurred in teaching in this decade. But it seemed useful to give a sense of the context in which they occurred, even though much of the above might better have been included in the following sections. The consolation for the reader is that those sections will consequently be shorter than otherwise.

The great challenge for IE during this decade was how to cope with the rate of expansion and increasing use of its ideas and materials, and there were also pervasive and long-lasting problems for IE in its new and successful growth. For example, it proved difficult to retrain many teachers, and for a couple of decades there remained a significant division in the teaching force between those that "got it" and those that didn't. Among those that didn't were some who seemed either unable to or positively unwilling to. IE, however — in a celebratory phrase that circulated on proponents' websites — was "out of the boutique."

The Curriculum: 2030–2040

There was much soul-searching within the educational establishment, and much pressure from without, about what was seen as the general ineffectiveness of the school as a socializing institution, at least in the ways explicit instruction was supposed to bring about. It was pointed out that if someone at age twenty didn't know the function of the main social agencies of their community it wasn't because they were taught badly in the early years of schooling. That is, the socializing that was dealt with explicitly in the early Social Studies curriculum was increasingly seen to be ineffective and pointless and also intellectually trivial. Children were socialized by their families, peers, and communities well or badly, and the school's explicit contribution through Social Studies added so little that no one could measure it.

The claim by politicians and educational administrators that the schools had been failing to adequately socialize the young was especially galling to many teachers. The school in advanced societies had become the catch-all institution for problems with young people. The ecological crises had partly submerged for a while the racial crises in major cities in the West. The immigration policies adopted by these societies to supply their labor needs were not supported by the kinds of financing required to help the immigrants adapt to their new societies, and to educate the indigenous populations for the changes large-scale immigration inevitably and predictably brought with it. The impact on schooling in major cities was often devastating. In many cities, classrooms might have as many as a dozen languages represented among the students, none of them being the native language of the country. It was simply — and irresponsibly — assumed by those who created such policies that the resulting problems with regard to the young would be dealt with by the schools and that somehow someone would deal with educating students in such conditions. The politicians were responding to their economies' needs by importing high- and low-skilled labor, and they congratulated themselves on cheaply solving a crisis that their past underfunding of educational institutions had partly created.

So the school was put in an impossible situation, but its perceived failures led to administrators being open to trying some radical new "solutions" to regain public support. One solution derived from the suddenly fashionable IE ideas was the separation of academic activities from socializing activities. Such a separation had long been practiced in one form or another in most IE schools, and it was obvious that IE students were not any less adequately socialized than anyone else, and they did seem in general to be better educated.

That is, IE had pointed out that using academic achievements as determiners of social differentiation was inefficient all round: the anxiety connected with the social-sorting function interfered with academic activities, and such a use of academic results was a very inefficient way of performing the social-sorting function. But there was also a clear role for explicit socialization, and time should be made for it. It was not obvious, though, that the school was the best or even a good institution for this role. In the short term, though, no alternative was possible or economically feasible.

Toward the end of the decade the first attempts were made to separate the socializing program from the academic program on a wide scale. There was a de-emphasizing initially, and then a change of emphasis later, on grading in the academic program. The socialization program became subject to much more precise assessment procedures.

The first programs began by following a successful IE innovation in the previous decade, setting up a revised academic program in the mornings and a new kind of socializing program, including a revised Social Studies curriculum, and job preparation in the afternoons. Teachers chose which program they wanted to specialize in, and it was obvious to administrators that teachers on the whole made the choice with some relief and then performed better in their chosen contexts.

The afternoon activities were generally much more integrated into the society at large — they were seen anew as the integration of students into their varied social roles and as the preparation for a variety of possible jobs. More-refined instruments were developed for helping students focus on the kind of jobs they were interested in preparing for.

The School: 2030–2040

Some of the fearsome pressures on the school during this decade have already been indicated above. But the greatest pressure on the school during this decade came from the lower-middle and working classes which had long been its greatest supporters.

One justification that had been given for establishing the schools of the democratic states was that they would contribute to democratic social life. The schools would do this by providing "equality of opportunity" for all students. So the working-class child would no longer be ghettoized but would have an equal chance at attaining the same social goods the children of the rich had. Unfortunately, since the founding of the modern school, the most consistent, strong positive correlation was between students' eventual income level and cultural life and those of their parents. The school had signally failed to have any impact at all on this undemocratic and unjust class division. In defense, some school spokespeople claimed that there were many cases of shifts in income, education level, and class in the generations of families, but it was pointed out that during earlier centuries movement among classes had actually been greater in many places than it had since the schools were supposed to disrupt this undemocratic situation.

The publication in 2036 of Olmert's celebrated, or notorious, text *The Enemy of Social Progress: The Role of the Public School in Sustaining Class Barriers* was like a knife in the back for the educational establishment. Olmert claimed, and amassed statistics to prove, that modern schools had done more to prevent democratization of society than they had to contribute to it. That is, the school had become a greater agent in maintaining classes than the explicitly class-based societies that preceded its development.

To school personnel still imbued with progressivist ideas this was hard to take. Here they were being branded as one of societies' most regressive agencies while their commitments and self-definition asserted to themselves the opposite. For more than a century, school administrators and teachers had generally been, and perceived themselves to be, somewhat left-wing, socially sensitive, committed to equality of opportunity, and struggling on the front lines of the battle for social progress. Then this.

Like so many inconvenient facts this one had for a long time been largely ignored. That the school did nothing much to disrupt class patterns had simply become taken for granted and, indeed, used as an explanation and excuse for other inconvenient facts. Olmert pointed out that it was simply accepted that poorer students would perform less well on all kinds of tests. When some claimed that they were just being "realistic," Olmert used this as evidence that progressivism had given up the ghost. It was neither producing the academic results it had been promising from its beginning, nor showing evidence — given the social disruptions of states at the time — that schools were achieving their socializing roles adequately. Now Olmert put a final nail in the ideological coffin of progressivism by showing how the schools had been acting as enemies of social progress.

Of course, much of this was simplistic and inaccurate and some-times downright false, but the damage was widespread, and the educational establishment, whose members had rarely any philosophical training to deal with these attacks, was mostly running for cover.

The schools' failures to respond in a sensible way to social and ecological crises, the failures to improve scores in math, science, and literacy, and the recognition that the school was ineffective as an agency of social advancement for members of the working classes disappointed its main constituents. In that disappointment lay the demise of the school as it had been known from the mid-nineteenth century.

Conclusion

By the end of the decade the Third Way of educating was on the top of the agenda for educational administrators across the developed societies. Conferences, workshops, pre-service and in-service teacher education programs, curriculum guides, curriculum materials, and all the industry of educational change were at work to bring IE to more students. To the directors of IE, it seemed alternately as though they were in paradise and in dangerous waters, certain to lead to catastrophe. The change was too vast, the ideas were too complicated, the procedures for teaching required a transformation in teachers' sense of themselves and their role: it was exhilarating and fraught with anxiety and danger for the IE establishment. They reminded themselves that this unanticipated degree of success was what the gods provided before they destroyed you.

But finally IE was out from under progressivist attempts to co-opt its successes. IE schools finally were clearly recognized as different from the old-fashioned schools that had focused on procedural knowledge, how to do, how to find information, learning how to learn, child-centeredness, and its other dreary slogans. IE procedures promoted mastery of knowledge — that is, cognitive tools were developed only when significant knowledge, which was itself tied up with the cognitive tools, was learned. Even with such a tool as the story, it became activated in a sufficiently rich way only after students had learned stories from around the world, practiced their own storytelling techniques, received criticism, and revised their stories. They had to understand the tool in its many uses, and this required significant study, but it was a kind of study that nearly all children found they could do with some success and profit to themselves. The distinctive way in which IE aimed to engage and develop the imagination, emotions, and humor as crucial for adequate learning and understanding also became consistently emphasized, even if not always clearly understood or correctly implemented.

Through the educational turmoil of the decade, the spread of IE, from the perspective of those students who were its new recipients, had one single clear effect. The things they were now expected to do in school were interesting; their imaginations were engaged by the wonder of the world in which they found themselves. Even children who came to school from terrible social conditions could find some solace in the pleasure of the great adventure of the mind. Such an adventure doesn't solve social problems or heal personal distress or provide help for pain, but it opens up a door to a world that is full of wonder, and also full of the tools that can in time be turned to deal with the daily problems that beset us. One of the achievements of IE schools was that they didn't promise practical social benefits they could not deliver; IE promised only entry to a world of the mind that people could use as they wished in the practical and social worlds that surrounded them.

For many still encumbered with progressivist ideas, this change was the hardest to come to terms with. Instead of the school being a central agency, tied into social life, which determined what was relevant to students' educational needs, it was being transformed faster than many could keep up with into a place apart—a place where concern was focused on the mind and the accumulation of the cognitive tool kits that enhanced the power of minds.

During the 2040s many of the world's political and administrative personnel were embroiled in responding to twin problems. First, the continuing costly efforts to contain ecological damage remained a tense and uncertain struggle, and second, those efforts were both helped and hindered by the declining birthrate. Birthrates in the developed countries had been in decline for more than half a century, but in the 2040s the decline accelerated. Less-developed countries had only recently given evidence of the same trend, but coupled with diseases exacerbated by ecological damage and infrastructure decay, birthrates across the world began the first serious and sustained decline since modern humans evolved. In 2049 the average cohort of children entering into schools was less than three-quarters of the size of the graduating class.

In retrospect, of course, the declining birthrate was much less of a problem than was commonly feared at the time. But during the 2040s the administrators of school systems were absorbed with how to deal with fewer and fewer students. One result was a teaching population that was declining in numbers as its average age increased. Whether true or not — though in the vague form it was usually stated in it was a truism — the idea took hold that most of the crises facing the world had been caused more or less directly by inadequate education. Countries around the world significantly increased funding for education, and so teaching, with smaller classes and more money, became again an attractive profession. It also became a profession that began to attract large numbers of men. The new teachers, female and male, entering the schools by the latter part of the decade were among the best educated since the development of mass schooling.

Teaching: 2040–2050

Money being injected into education systems in significant amounts led to more opportunities for in-service teachers to receive further academic study and methodological expertise. To indicate some of the main changes that affected teachers and their practice during this period, selections from a log kept by Patrick Piatrowski in Clonmel, Ireland, in 2049 will be used. Mr. Piatrowski had been accepted into a one-semester program of professional upgrading, and the log includes various papers he wrote for the courses he took and includes also his own reflections on, and description of, the program — which is what makes it useful for present purposes. He had become a primary school teacher seven years earlier.

The first excerpt is from the document he was asked to write as a part of his application for the program, giving reasons why he should be accepted into it.

After five years of teaching, which according to all accounts has been successful, and which I have felt quite good about in general, I nevertheless feel some misgivings in front of my classes. I tend to use IE methods fairly extensively, having been comprehensively trained in their use and having found them to work well in my own practice, but there is a sense that they are at the root of the misgivings I feel as much as a benefit to me. That is, the techniques of moving toward the ideals of IE — of "engaging students' imaginations in learning about the world," as the textbook kept saying — did make the daily tasks of teaching rewarding, as I saw my pupils working well and being genuinely engaged in their learning most of the time, but even so, I increasingly felt I wasn't getting at the core of the topics I was teaching.

Hard to express it clearly, but if I was teaching about, say, birds of prey to my six-year-olds, I'd prepare materials on owls as "the huge silent killers of the night sky" and all the rest of it and arrange all the I-net resources they needed, and it would certainly keep them engaged and learning. But I kept having a sense that IE principles called for more — more depth of understanding, a wider and richer understanding of the complex cycles of predation and survival in nature, more of the physical feelings of the owl launching silently from a branch toward the tiny vole scurrying in the grass. Yes, I know it is always possible to find deeper understanding and that one has to settle sometimes for adequate rather than richer imaginative engagement. But the IE ideals I had taken on board were in danger of shipwrecking me, making me dissatisfied with what I was achieving.

Now it is easy to overdramatize this. I was mostly content and felt competent, but what was initially a small undercurrent of slight discomfort became a wider dissatisfaction. My hope is that the program will help me either better identify and deal with this dissatisfaction and/or will equip me with the further tools and techniques I need to teach in a manner closer to the IE ideals that I share. Either way, I hope to emerge a more secure and better teacher.

Clearly those who decided admittance to the program found this part of Mr. Piatrowski's application appealing. The following personal reflection, at the end of his second week of the program, gives some sense of its overall structure.

I had thought the two days of discussion and analysis at the beginning was a bit of a waste of time, but I suppose it has proved well spent as they have tailored the program for each of us in the group. [The program was built around cohorts of fifteen. The discussion and analysis he mentions were largely based on the portfolio he had submitted in his application package.] The main decision they made concerned the proportion of academic to methodological work we need. My program was split 75% academic and 25% methodological—though, in fact, they were far from as distinct as this suggests. From the first week or so of the classes and workshops, it seems they think I need to spend more time on learning how to abstract from topics the key features that will engage my pupils' cognitive tool kits. And that means I need to know more about them. My three main classes are History for Primary Schools, Science for Primary Schools, and Math for Primary Schools.

The subjects are taught to us using IE principles, so we are constantly exercising precisely the methods we ourselves need to use with our pupils. The instructors focus on the curriculum materials we have to teach and deepen our understanding of the particular history, science, or math topics but also bring out as they do so those features that can most powerfully engage us, as well as showing the features that will appeal particularly to our pupils. We are looking at each topic from mythic, romantic, and philosophic perspectives all the time. I thought this would be confusing, especially as I have been trained mostly in mythic tool use, but I am finding already that the ability to shift perspectives more easily is improving my ability to think of alternative mythic procedures.

The science instructor, Ms. Zazkis, is really helpful. She began discussing principles of how to focus on a topic to bring out the emotionally engaging qualities and some affective images. Toward the end of the class we dealt with one of the topics I teach each spring: whales. "What's the story about whales?" she asked. "They are big," one of the women said. "And some sing," said Ms. Zazkis. We sat in silence for a minute wondering what we were supposed to do with that. "They are mammals that spend their life swimming," I said, a bit cautiously. It was the kind of observation that seemed to fit in with hers; maybe we'd get to see better what she was getting at. "Good," she smiled, to my relief. But good what? I wondered. "The blue whale is the biggest animal that has ever existed on earth, and can make the loudest sounds," said the guy next to me. "Good," again from Ms. Zazkis. "Some whales travel more than 12,000 miles a year," said Marnie, the woman I'd met on the first day at the social. "The heart of a typical blue whale weighs about a thousand pounds and is the size of a small car," added Ms. Zazkis. Then she asked again, "So what's the story about whales?" She paused for a minute, then added, "A loud human shout can hit around 70 decibels, a jet engine hits around 140 decibels, but a whale can reach nearly 190 decibels. They can be heard for hundreds of miles at sea. And our story is . . .?"

"They are amazing?" tentatively asked another man at the end of the table.

"Aren't we all?" she smiled. "So is the mouse amazing. Perhaps we might compare those two amazing animals? But first, *feel* about whales. What images come to your mind? Can you feel the sound of that great heart throbbing in the ocean? Think of it sending pondfuls of blood pounding through its great arteries — like tunnels through which you could crawl. The graceful rolling of that mighty bulk? Their bare survival from hunters earlier in the century? Their brains can weigh twenty pounds — what are they thinking; how do they think? Their strange history — of hoofed land animals returning to the sea, breathing air and giving birth to their young like other mammals, but in the water? Their vast journeys through all the oceans of our watery planet?" She paused again. "It is night. A huge storm is creating forty-foot waves, lightning flashes and tearing thunder rolls not far above two blue whales. They rise up to see the black water illuminated for a second and then plunge deep for half an hour at a time, then rise again into the turbulent air to breathe, then their great bodies sink down again. They are keeping a steady twenty miles an hour. They are a mile apart and keep in constant touch with low clicking sounds from one to the other. They are heading from off the coast of South America to the rich feeding grounds that will soon bloom off the south of Australia. What are they thinking and feeling about the black waves that throw even their mighty bodies about? What compulsions are driving them on such a vast voyage, and how do they find their way through the featureless waters? What are they saying to each other in the turbulent night?"

She looked at the clock at that point and said, "Homework. What's the story on whales?" And then she left.

[Excerpt from a week later.]

Ms. Zazkis again. We now have five different units on whales for second graders developed by our small groups. None of them is like the one I have been teaching for a few years. I worked on two, both of which she said were good. The unit I taught in the past relied a lot on I-net resources: video of whales at sea, 3-D pictures of their skeletons, and realistic diagrammatic videos of their bodies' functions. I did a section on "whale records," looking at the biggest whales, and then the smallest, the loudest, fastest, deepest divers, biggest brains, longest migrations, most stable group structure. Even though most of the pupils I teach are probably "mythic," I included this for those already moving to, and encouraging the others to move to, more romantic tools. She thought that section worth keeping, though suggesting I might change some of the categories a bit to bring out their emotional possibilities — so the "group structure" might be better investigated in terms of most and least sociable, or loneliest and most gregarious. She suggested the category of the deadliest, which I had actually used before, but forgot to include. Also she suggested a set of "records" based on their songs. The longest, most complex, most poignant, each pupil's favorite — "and then ask them why they like it so."

The new unit she spent the most time with, done by Marnie's group, was called "The Noises of Whales." I thought that wasn't a particularly vivid way of engaging pupils with the topic, but it began with a male humpback's song that was very haunting. And then they discussed recent interpretations of whale songs and the range of things whales communicated about. They had a section on the loudest animal that ever lived rather than the usual biggest animal, though they got to its size through the noises. Then they had an audio image of the heartbeat of a blue whale made by a tracer-microphone that had passed through its bloodsteam recording as it went. They had sounds of whales breaching and described what they were doing. They managed to cover all the information about whales that is part of the usual curriculum through their sounds, even recordings of whales traveling at different speeds and in cold and warm water, with oscilloscope images. They showed hardly any video material, and used very few pictures. Ms. Zazkis complimented them on their ingenuity and the engagement and education of pupils' hearing.

My group's unit was called "The Mysterious Giant" and focused first on how little we understood about the blue whale. It is hard to give pupils a sense of the scale of these animals, so we began with a lightweight replica of a whale's tongue, which we were just able to squeeze into the classroom. It had the texture of a whale's tongue, and we explained that a real tongue would weigh about four tons! It had taken a number of us a week to make, and we were very proud of it. She said it was impressive, but wondered where we planned to store it in our classroom or in the school. We hadn't really thought of that. Then we focused on the mystery of animals' size, and why any creature would get to be as big as a blue whale. This led to the amount it needed to eat, and how it ate, and so on. By focusing on the mysteries that remain about the blue whale — its migration patterns, methods of navigation, senses of feeding grounds, emotional life, intelligence, and so on — we tried to engage students' attraction to puzzles. (We drew on Herbert Spencer's proposal that the huge brain of many whales was bigger than was necessary for the normal functioning of a nonrational animal and was likely connected with a very vivid emotional life. We then looked at more recent evidence on this topic.) We worked from the sense of mystery towards the more "romantic" sense of awe that these animals can so easily stimulate in pupils.

The unit I did by myself was a comparison between a pygmy mouse and a blue whale — which she had half jokingly suggested a week or so ago. I did a detailed comparison of various of their bodily features and functions, and made it more engaging by giving each of my two animals individual characters and had them take part in the comparisons the unit was based on. So the "teacher" was hardly present for this unit, as it was entirely "taught" by the mouse and whale. I also showed all the mouse pictures in large scale and the whale pictures in small.

By the end of the semester I had learned a great deal of math, science, and history related to the curriculum area I was teaching. It was clearly the case, as I had been taught in my IE teacher education program, that the more one knew about a subject the easier it was to become imaginatively engaged by it. It also was useful constantly to be thinking and learning in a context in which the underlying cognitive tools of imaginative engagement were constantly being made explicit to us. It made it so much easier for us to be able to identify what tools we wanted to engage and to find the appropriate knowledge to be able to do so.

We might conclude this section by considering a brief segment of a later part of his log.

In some ways the most useful part of the program for me was the weekly hour-long meetings we had with Mr. Gobunka about helping our second-year pupils with their portfolios. These are the topics they study from year one to the end of their schooling. I had been doing this fairly routinely with my set of pupils, finding them additional resources, suggesting further dimensions of their topic that they could explore, and generally being as supportive as I could. The analysis of my teaching that had come into the program with me, and that had formed the basis for the structuring of my program, showed that I had a problem getting to a level of understanding of the material to really engage many of my students' mythic cognitive tools. (It seems I was better at using some romantic ones, but I often used them a little early and at the cost of fuller development of the mythic.)

Walter Gobunka gave me a set of year-two portfolios on a number of topics — I had one on paper, one on African head gear, games played with balls, rivers, apple varieties and history, and silver. He asked me to examine each of the portfolios, comment on how well they had been begun in year one, and then make suggestions for what the pupils should do next. I started with the portfolio on apples. The pupil had drawn red and green apples, quite well, and indicated that one was a McIntosh and the other a Granny Smith. Then there was a list of apple varieties. The first part of the list was composed from the varieties the pupil had found in shops, and then she had added some extra ones that grew locally that weren't in the shops. Then there was a more elaborate list, clearly pulled from the I-net, but the pupil had made some additional notes next to those she had eaten — notes about size and color and taste. She had a five-star system to indicate which she thought best. She noted that her list included less than a hundredth of the 7,500 varieties that currently are cultivated around the world. There was a file on apple history, which included pieces about the earliest sweet and flavorful apples, such as those we eat today, being first identified in Kazakhstan many thousands of years ago. She had a map identifying the area, and also a world map with small notes indicating places where there were very old records of apples.

Mr. Gobunka asked me what I'd suggest for the pupil's next assignment that would perhaps do a better job of drawing on and developing some of her mythic tools. I suggested a file be opened on stories about apples: the Bible story, though it mentions only "fruit," is usually assumed to involve an apple; the Swiss story of William Tell shooting the apple off his son's head; the story of John Chapman, better known as "Johnny Appleseed"; the story of Newton's falling apple; and so on. I also mentioned some games and verses and sayings about apples, and working out what " 'the apple of my eye" means, or "One rotten apple spoils the whole barrel," and why people say "An apple a day keeps the doctor away."

His initial response was a bit like Rita Zazkis's. He said "Good," but I didn't get the sense of there being much enthusiasm in it. "Think of some of the other tools year-two pupils have available for use and development. And remember that apple trees are part of the rose family. The biggest apple was around four pounds. Why do apples float? The current Lady apple was first cultivated by an Etruscan called Api, and in France it is still called 'pomme d'Api' — a good way to be remembered. The Greeks and Romans prized apples and knew about twenty varieties. There are now around 7,500 varieties cultivated worldwide. What's the story about apples?"

By this time I was ready to punch the next person who asked me "What's the story about whatever." Not an appropriate academic response, I know. I realize it wasn't the question that was the problem, but how hard I found it to answer. And I also realized that's what they had identified as my main weakness and that's why they kept throwing the question at me. Also I was beginning to feel a bit intimidated by the mountains of information all the instructors seemed to have about every topic raised. I suppose they had been doing this for a while, and maybe they just knew about the set of topics commonly taught to pupils at the ages teachers like me dealt with.

I suggested that the pupil might focus on how the few varieties known in the ancient world grew to be so many today. It seemed a bit mysterious to me. "Yes, that's possible," Mr. Gobunka said. "But think about images, feel for some vivid images, and what binary opposites can you locate in the topic? What wonder and mystery?"

I remembered suddenly W. B. Yeats's "glimmering girl / With apple blossom in her hair" and Wandering Aengus who had looked for her for so long and thought when he had found her that they would pluck "till time and times were done / the silver apples of the moon, the golden apples of the sun." I mentioned it hesitantly, but Mr. Gobunka smiled and said, "Well, she is only six years old. Do you think she could make sense of the poem?"

"She will make a six-year-old's sense of it," I said, "but there is so much magic and mystery in the poem, and the rhyme and rhythm are so magical that it could add a dimension to her sense of apples that would likely engage and develop her tool of mystery. It could set up resonances that will stay with her for the rest of her life.'Poetry is a supertool,' you said to me a few weeks back! And it is one of the nearly perfect poems in English."

"Mr. Piatrowski, you and W. B. Yeats have just succeeded in your assignment. You see,'the story' can be found in directions we had not at first thought about. Planning teaching really is like telling a story or writing a poem: let the mind play around the topic, explore varied forms of information, but then trust to those things that flicker to the surface of your mind for a moment here and there. Teaching as storytelling, eh?"

The documents relating to Mr. Piatrowski's subsequent teaching once he returned to his school suggest that the program worked well for him. The pattern of his program was not unlike the general emphasis on educating new teachers in IE procedures. Teaching now required a masters degree and then a two-year teacher education program, one half of which at least was given over to course work in the topics that would form the individual student's teaching specialty. The teachers' own passion for the subject, it was constantly pointed out, was the main stimulus to students' learning, so there was much emphasis laid on bringing out the romantic dimension of the knowledge first. The tools used in teaching in these programs, as Mr. Piatrowski experienced, were the tools teachers would later use themselves in teaching, consequently making it easier for them to feel their effectiveness.

The Curriculum: 2040–2050

Many subtle and some not-so-subtle changes began to become routine in the curriculum as IE ideas about how knowledge grows in children's minds increasingly displaced the old progressivist "cognitive developmental" views. Progressivist ideas, as we have seen, represented young children as intellectually incompetent: "concrete" thinkers, "pre-operational," "pre-rational," only able to use forms of thought that were embryonic forms of adult thinking, unable to learn any content that involved abstractions, capable only of thinking tied to their local environment and experience, and so on. These progressivist ideas had contributed greatly to trivializing the primary curriculum, at a time when children's intelligences were most active in their use of certain important cognitive tools. The increasing dominance of IE ideas opened up a radical rethinking of the primary curriculum.

One of the less-subtle innovations followed what had been the successful practice of many IE schools for a couple of decades. They had claimed that young children's education would benefit from study and gradual mastery of an "exotic" language, that is, a language distant from the student's native language, and preferably one that was "dead," or not used routinely today. Latin, Middle Chinese, Greek, and Sanskrit were popular choices, but where the resources were available, aboriginal languages from countries around the world were also brought to life in modern children's experience. IE schools stated a preference for languages whose written form was different from that of the children's native orthography, but the availability of teachers was one obvious constraining factor on the choices available — though study of "exotic" languages became common for students who intended to become teachers.

When the practice was first introduced into IE schools, many progressivists had claimed that it was a foolish innovation, because only a tiny minority of children would be able to learn one of these languages, and anyway there was no point or utility in such an exercise. The IE response was that the utility criterion belonged in the "socialization" curriculum, but their introduction of an exotic language was there for educational reasons. They also argued that part of the reason that Greek and Latin used to be taught so badly in the nineteenth century was due to their having been taught initially for utilitarian reasons — for church and law careers — and in the twentieth century because, in the dwindling locations in which they persisted, no adequate justification was given. As a result they were taught largely as strings of rules, much like mathematics, but without even the marginal utilitarian justifications given for teaching math.

One argument used for this innovation was that a language is like an eye on the world; it brings certain features of the world into a particular perspective, in some degree shaped by the language learned — languages are not "innocent eyes" on reality. Given that belief, it was argued that the more distinct the second language was from the first, the greater and deeper the dimensions of the world that could be seen and understood. The argument was made that languages served in some degree analogously to our eyes: a single eye giving a two-dimensional view of the world, with the second eye allowing a third dimension. So, it was felt, the wider apart the languages were, the richer the understanding they yielded at some basic level. It should be mentioned that there was nothing in the basic IE theory to support this practice of introducing exotic languages, but something about the culture of IE schooling made it appeal to a generation of IE principals.

More-hardheaded teachers and professors of education argued the absurdity of such a procedure for children who were having difficulty enough in mastering their own language and forms of literacy. They argued that less-able children would find the exotic language simply too hard and be totally discouraged, and it would also interfere with what learning they could manage.

But nearly all children, it was found, could learn these languages in significant, though varying, degree; well enough for it to have become clear how much seeing the world through a language quite different from their native language added to the flexibility of their understanding of their world and experience. With the developments of IE pedagogy, and the removal of learning the languages from the business of determining future jobs and life chances, children displayed much greater pleasure and ability in mastering these languages than progressivist assumptions had predicted. And, unsurprisingly to IE supporters, these students' ability to deal with their native language and literacy was improved by their engagement with an exotic language.

The middle of the decade also saw the introduction of the first separate buildings dedicated to distinct academic and socializing activities. This was a fraught innovation, opposed even by many within the IE movement. They argued that the distinction between socializing and academic activities was not so great as to merit different institutions, and that there was considerable conceptual unclarity in the distinction between them. That conceptual unclarity, they asserted, would guarantee practical difficulties whose confusions would lead to problems as bad as those the separation of functions was supposed to solve.

In nearly all schools in which IE had gained significant influence, which was by now most, some separation between the academic and socializing activities was evident. So in some schools there might be "literacy for life and work" and also "literacy for the mind," "useful history" — that is "our" story — and also "useless history," as the focus on developing a historical consciousness was called, ironically, by teachers and students alike. The humor of these names became a marked feature of the new IE schooling. There was certainly seriousness of purpose, but it was lightened by humor because, some argued, those in the system no longer felt a deep uncertainty and insecurity about what they were supposed to be doing. That uncertainty had led to a generally rather humorless approach to educating in the past. Maybe the recognized aim of ironic understanding added to the general acceptance of a certain lightness of tone in the new education.

Similarly such schools would have separate classes on "science for everyday life" and "the scientific worldview."

This brought out some of the limits and problems of the distinction between the socializing and academic aims. Literacy for life versus literacy for its own sake clearly overlapped. At one level it seemed to some that the distinction was unworkable, but it quickly became clear that the topics of the past curriculum could be relatively easily divided up as fitting better in one area than another, and where there seemed some overlap, the overlap was fairly straightforwardly accepted and dealt with by casual agreements among the teachers. Separating them also made clearer for the teachers just what their purpose was and how best they might achieve those aims. When they had been mixed together, there had always been confusion of purpose. So matters of utility, the rules of polite messaging, appropriate language, grammatical structure, and so on, were made easier for the "socializing" teachers. Similarly the "academic" teachers concentrated instead on the development of individuals' "voice" and style; poetry became increasingly popular, and poets found a new source of income from the patronage of academic programs.

The areas of confusion where the distinction seemed not to work well quickly led to joint projects. This unexpected ease of accommodation was a reflection of a deeper ease achieved between the teachers in the two institutions. There had been a lot of concern expressed, as the socializing/academic distinction began to be increasingly institutionalized, that there would be competition and conflict between the two kinds of school. Of great concern to those administering the system was the expectation that academic-school teaching would be more highly esteemed, and the socializing-school teachers would be considered second rate. There had been much policy debate about paying socializing-school teachers more to compensate for the expected loss of status and to ensure that good candidates were attracted to socializing schooling. But it seems fair to say, the almost universal expectation of difference in esteem between academic and socializing teachers quite quickly worked out almost opposite to what nearly everyone expected.

The grounds for the improved status of socializing teachers were set in their teacher education programs. Typically, in the two-year programs now mandated, the students destined for socializing and academic schools worked in common for the first half-year, learning generic skills and trying them out in supervised school settings. Thereafter the two sets of students increasingly followed different streams. Those electing preparation for teaching in socializing schools had in some ways the harder training. The procedures of IE had become prominent in both areas of the program, but engaging students' imaginations in learning the more utilitarian features of language required more skill and effort than engaging them in literature, it was assumed. Because of this assumption, unexpectedly, those graduating from socializing teacher-education programs carried the halo effect of being more skilled. Combined with the higher status due to their increased successes in ensuring better-equipped citizens able to handle the increasingly sophisticated tasks facing the young adult in 2040s and 2050s society, this aura of considerable skill at performing the harder task entirely offset what some had predicted would be the continuing privileging of those dealing with the academic. In addition, though, the academic teachers also benefited from the aura of the traditional world of academic pursuits. The result over the following decades was what two centuries earlier in an English government Act had been called "parity of esteem." It had not been achieved among the schools in 1940s and 1950s England because the schooling was unequal and the outcomes for the students in the different schools was unequal, but in the mid-twenty-first century, it was the same students attending both kinds of school, and the achievements of both sets of teachers was generally valued equally but for different reasons.

Socializing-school curricula were determined by best estimates of the knowledge and skills students would need to survive and succeed in the social world that awaited them. Academic-school curricula were increasingly determined by the IE principle of what knowledge would best help the development of the appropriate tool kits of understanding.

Evaluation procedures in each kind of institution diverged quite quickly. In socializing schools much more precise evaluative procedures were developed. Because the aim of socializing schooling was now much more precise — teaching and learning focused on citizenship, social value, and utility — there were much clearer criteria for testing of various kinds. In academic schools, though, evaluation procedures tended to largely disappear till the end of schooling. By then students' future directions into further education, training, or jobs was in some part determined by the socializing-school evaluations. Those competing for academic institutions and further training went through a ten-day evaluation process in the summer of completing their schooling. Some of this involved presenting their portfolios for separate evaluation and doing some traditional examinations, but much of it was made up of interviews about the students' interests and background, and discussion and assessment of their ambitions, and so on. Students' articulateness and clarity in expressing their interests, combined with their portfolios and other written materials, allowed selection based on varied criteria relevant to academic potential.

The other curriculum change, which teachers from a century or half century earlier would have found unfamiliar, was the construction of large-scale narratives into which the required curriculum content was fitted. While this had been common in IE schools for some time, its general effectiveness made it almost universal during this decade. Commonly teachers would plan together in year cohorts and decide together on the general narrative themes they would explore during the year. Many successful themes were available on IE websites, but, frequently, local issues could form the basis for a successful narrative, especially in socializing schools. Curricula were built on large narratives that spanned much of the year, with other narratives playing roles within them. So in one case in Argentina, in an area where there was a major wind-farm generating electric power, teachers decided that the fourth-grade narrative would be wind. During the year they ensured that the whole curriculum, in both socializing and academic schools, built their lessons on the overall "story" of the movement of the air around the planet. In science lessons they learned about atmospheric pressure, exploring it through the heroes who had first discovered why the air moved, causing wind; in mathematics they studied volume, so they could begin to map mathematically the movement of prevailing winds; in history they discovered forms of transport that depended on wind and followed the great Chinese and European voyages of discovery; in geography they mapped the prevailing winds around the world and studied their past and present impact on landforms and on the movement of water; and so on. By the end of the year, owing to the richness of their understanding of wind and a thousand other things they had learned about movements of the air, students had accumulated knowledge and understanding that would remain with them to the end of their lives.

The School: 2040–2050

By the end of the decade, a visitor from fifty years earlier would have immediately noticed significant differences on entering a new school. The visitor would first have been taken aback to see two different buildings — even if physically connected on the same site, as was commonly the case — both claiming to be schools. The curriculum of each was significantly different from the other; in one, the latest technologies would be evident, and in the other, hardly any technology would be visible, except the screens built into desk surfaces, over which an opaque cover was usually in place.

Many educators from a half century earlier would have expected the presence of technology in the socializing school, but would have been puzzled by its near absence from the academic schools. "Access to information" had been one of the mantras of the early days, when computers began to have an effect on education. But access to knowledge had never been the problem, and it should have been clear then, and was to many, of course. Even a hundred years earlier, students had access to plenty of knowledge; the problem was getting it into the students, and getting it to mean anything much to them. The most fundamental change in schooling was tied up with precisely that problem. Technology had its uses in providing immediate access to any information required, but the more important feature of the new schooling was the recognition of how to use the older technologies of human communication like the story and mental images, which connect knowledge with human emotions. It was this more profound revolution that IE had delivered in transforming the school — a transformation that was achieved at a remarkable pace during the 2040s. They were ever afterward referred to as "the years of the revolution in education."

There were those who claimed that IE's success, while seemingly serendipitous, was inevitable by some route or other, simply because of its practical success at the classroom level.

Conclusion

Throughout this chapter the term *IE* has been used. This has been in some degree a convenience to indicate the package of educational ideas and practices that became more popular throughout this period, and whose development to this dominant position within education has been traced through the previous chapters. But the name *IE* itself began to disappear during the 2030s, and by the time the ideas became, as it were, the default educational beliefs, the word *imaginative* had largely disappeared. People talked about "modern" education or the "new forms" of education, while some did still use *IE*, of course. In part *IE* retained some currency because of the corporations that produced materials and ideas to assist teachers in implementing the approach in academic and socializing programs in all curriculum areas for all ages. The corporations, perhaps conservatively, used *IE* in their names.

Among the developments that seem not worth exploring in detail here are the divisions that developed within IE. It was not without irony, as the book *Fragmented Imaginative Education* perhaps exaggeratedly claimed, that it was possible to identify distinctive Salernoist strains of IE and prominent progressivist strains. The book was generally thought to have overstated the degree of fragmentation, but it was certainly the case that distinctive IE approaches were pursued in different places. Each developed its own research and development centers, and each was serviced by a number of corporations making materials and lesson aids available to teachers.

The divisions and continuing disagreements, however, were more about matters of procedure and implementation and only marginally about the ends and purposes of education. Education had become more like health, as a concept generally understood and agreed on. There remained disputes about health care, but they were not about what it means to be healthy. The problem for education for so long had been precisely fundamental disputes about what it meant to be educated. Increasingly, with a generally accepted and persuasive concept of education in place, all parts of the education system could work more efficiently and effectively.

eight

2050–2060

In this final chapter, rather than follow the divisions of the earlier chapters, I will draw a brief picture of education during the 2050s.

Teaching, the Curriculum, and the School

With the birth of a baby, the caregivers were given materials and guides to developing the infant's somatic understanding. (In this text, the terms *somatic, mythic, romantic, philosophic,* and *ironic* have been preserved for the sake of consistency, even though those terms, and the general five-part structure of IE, fell into disuse after the theoretical developments of IE during the 2030s. The terms, always a source of some discontent and confusion, were replaced by a more adequate vocabulary. In the appendix to this work are included all the various and changing terms deployed during the half century covered in this history.) Education came to be seen as a life-long process. Earlier in the century this phrase had been used to suggest that more attention should be given to the needs of older learners, and this did indeed occur, but more important was the recognition that all subsequent education was dependent on a sound foundation in the earliest years.

One danger that was evident in the programs for babies developed earlier in the century was the increasingly early introduction of the "industrialization" processes that had done so much to deprive children and youth of pleasure in the schools of the previous century. That danger was largely averted in the new IE programs available during the 2050s because of their emphasis on the development of humor as a crucial part of all education, especially in the earliest years. It had become clear that the peek-a-boo games and their endless variants, played with humor, were vital precursors to the intellectual developments that sustained individuals in good mental health for the six-score-years-and-ten of the average life span. And humor and love are allied "tools" in children's upbringing.

The mind's tool kit for grasping the world, which had earlier been interpreted in terms of the senses, its musicality, rhythm and pattern, and so on, was also the subject of the guides that parents received. Each of these "sensory tools" was tied in particular to games that could be played with babies in the natural world, and much emphasis was laid on simply letting the infants experience natural phenomena and giving them time to, for example, put a foot in a stream and feel the water and observe how it responded to the foot being moved. (Parents had done such things for millennia, of course, but too many parents did not understand how crucial this kind of activity was for future intellectual growth.)

The other major part of the tool kit of the body is its emotions. The materials parents received with their new baby also included much guidance on the development of the emotions, and, of course, on the control of their own. The importance of reliable loving relationships for future emotional development was underlined, and significant financial support was available to provide more time for caregiver-infant interactions. It had become only too clear that a small investment by the state in the support of parents reaped huge savings in crime reduction within a short time.

The infant's senses were also drawn to the sounds of the natural world, to regularities in those sounds, and to rhythm and music of varying kinds, particularly the music and rhythms that can be made by the human voice and body. Soundscapes generated by animals' voices, and by single instruments, then groups of instruments, were provided to help train the ear to increasing sensitivity to more subtle patterns of sound.

With the development of oral language, and what used to be called mythic understanding, the rhythms could elaborate into rhymes. The sense of mystery that comes with our consciousness could find new outlets in Mother Goose and orally told "myth" stories from the traditions of cultures from around the world. Parents were encouraged to *tell* stories to young children rather than read them or allow media presentations. The familiar loving voice and the warmth of bodily contact set the conditions for the generation of children's unique mental images as they listened to stories and rhymes. Certain sets of stories, which were provided to parents for telling, were chosen for their encouragement of particularly rich image-generation and, connectedly, their emotional power. These stories often took the form of extended jokes. Again, much emphasis was given to the development of the child's sense of humor, both through oral forms — stories and jokes — but also in the more elaborate games now available to them, and in the beginnings of ironic interactions.

Once children went to school they were increasingly introduced to "the great stories of human cultural history," that is, they learned about how we, as a species, came to discover the world around us, and the sky above us; how language developed and what we can do with it; how we learned to use scientific approaches to discovering the nature of things. These lessons were built on the tools we have seen earlier — using binary opposites, metaphors, story structures, and so on. In introducing the water cycle, for example, teachers would encourage children to imagine they were a woman or man sitting on a hill overlooking the mouth of a great river pouring into the sea four thousand years earlier, wondering where all that incessantly flowing water was going to. How could they make sense of it? Maybe it poured over a vast waterfall somewhere, into an abyss at the end of the world? What was the story about how people in fact came to work out what was happening?

One of the more dramatic innovations of the previous decade — the separate buildings for academic and socializing schooling — oddly enough became increasingly less common in this decade. Once the division and separate purposes of various educational activities had been recognized, it proved relatively straightforward to go about schooling such that requiring separate buildings seemed an excessive response. Distinctive forms of teacher training did remain in place with the different emphases, but it was suggested that as people became better educated, and society itself could be seen as better educated, the notion of socializing increasingly took on aspects of what in the past might have been seen more exclusively as academic school activities.

More straightforward socializing and personal development matters were increasingly pushed out of the school, and aspects of socializing schools began to be hived off into other social agencies dealing with young people. It was as though, at last, after nearly two hundred years of state-sponsored schooling, educational authorities realized that the best contribution they could make to the state was simply to educate children. Much of the earlier trouble, it was now seen, was that the school was set up too deliberately to be a training institution for the state's needs. As such it attracted people whose main interest was social engineering and indoctrination — political or religious or some other form — and who conceived of education as the process in which students accepted the appropriate doctrines and political and social belief systems. This was as true in what were considered the liberal democratic states as in the totalitarian states.

One of the most influential books of the early 2050s drew on a slogan used for different purposes in the previous century: *Just say NO*. The "no" was to anyone who tried to see the school as appropriately involved in activities other than stimulating, elaborating, and developing the cognitive tools and kinds of understanding of students. The "no," relatedly, was also to any conception of education that tried to introduce ideas of educating other than maximizing for each student the array of cognitive tools and kinds of understanding available. (This didn't solve all educational problems and arguments, of course, but it did at last mean that education was conceived of as having a single aim, to which all educational workers could direct their efforts. This theoretical achievement led to a huge practical relief to the administrators of school systems.)

So the schools that children attended were profoundly different from any that had existed in the previous century. In the past, the states' leaders, from the most conscientious liberal democrats to the most ruthless dictators, seemed unable to see the school systems they inherited, which the state paid for, as something other than institutions that should serve their interests. State leaders' interests were never simply in educating children, but always, first, in the forms of socialization they desired. Given that, pretty well everyone thought they had an equal right to speak with authority on education. Now education had become a process of developing somewhat distinctive kinds of understanding, and the need for some expertise in grasping how these kinds of understanding were constructed from arrays of cognitive tools made education an area in which specialized knowledge was important. The new schools and their organization came more to resemble health care, as I noted above. Politicians and other interest groups did not feel they could casually speak with authority about details of health care, and now the same was felt to be the case about education.

During the next few years of the typical student's schooling in the 2050s, the curriculum and teaching gradually moved from using most prominently the tool kit of oral language and introduced increasingly those tools that literacy and the ways it has been most fully exploited in human cultures incline the mind to use. The new tool kit did not displace the earlier one entirely, and it also was attentive to the general tools that would later become more prominent. While this all seemed complex and perhaps too difficult for everyday planning and teaching, the principles were not so difficult in practice, and there were also many resources and supports available for teachers. So the students moved increasingly into an approach to learning about the world and experience through heroes, the extremes of reality, and the array of hopes, fears, and passions that have driven human achievements and the generation of knowledge.

These "romantic" years included puberty for most young people, and their explorations of the world through the curriculum tried to show it as turbulent, passionate, and fearful as their own shifting moods. The portfolios that each student had begun in their first year of schooling often became an area of obsessive interest during these years, and tutors oversaw its growth and deepening in many dimensions. It had been anticipated earlier that this would also be the period when many students would revolt against their portfolio study and abandon it as a sign of a system with which they felt disaffected, but oddly this rarely happened. In cases where students went through more turbulent experiences of puberty, the portfolio was seen most commonly as their place of security, their own place to which they could retreat against those features of the world they felt oppressed or depressed by. What sometimes happened, even for a matter of years, was that students continued to work on their portfolios but would not share them with tutors or families. Sometimes close friends began to work together, making connections between their portfolio topics and developing a common strand in each of their portfolios. The schools supported many varied forms of portfolio development.

The tools mentioned earlier were built on and developed as students explored the human and natural worlds in more detail. Often the curricula were somewhat chaotic by the standards of the previous century — students were allowed to follow particular interests in great detail and to neglect what earlier might have been considered a more proportionate study of different subject areas. Teachers were encouraged to recognize the individual nature of wonder and to let it lead students when it appeared. Of course, the teachers were also trained in evoking the wonder in each topic, but each student did not respond equally however well the teachers did their job. Much of the curriculum, in science and math no less that in history and the arts, was seen constantly through the transcendent human qualities of those who discovered the knowledge or who used it with living passion. Those transcendent qualities — of compassion, energy, ingenuity, courage, fear, tenacity, and so on and on — became tools that both humanized the meaning of the content being studied but also extended students' understanding of such qualities within themselves.

Humor remained a part of the schooling of "romantic" students, but it took on a new form as literacy developed. The jokes that tended to become most engaging either had a scatological bent or were sufficiently risqué for them to not make good classroom fodder — the old "ghost"/"goat" kind of jokes. Jokes about deeply embarrassing situations also increasingly appealed, as did jokes that played rather more wildly with language and presumed a wider social knowledge: "What's

Irish and sits in your garden?" "Pati O'Furniture." "How do you stop a snake from striking?" "Pay it a decent wage," and, groaningly, so on. A kind of counterromantic response tended to find an outlet in sarcasm. So tolerance of slightly wilder forms of humor was evident during schooling in those years. And teachers were trained not to be reluctant to use the kind of wit that adds perhaps critical commentary and low comedy to what might otherwise be somewhat staid.

The curriculum and the class groupings were much more varied in both the time allotted for them and the numbers of students who would come together for any particular "class" than was the case in the schools of the previous century. Some classes—on people, or the technology of everyday things, or ideas—were organized in quarter-hour segments, sufficient only to grasp the romantic features of the topic, to stimulate interest. Bite-sized topics simply opened up possibilities that might in some other context be explored at greater length, or ignored. The aim of those smaller curriculum segments was to open up moments of wonder about the world and human experience, or to show extraordinary human qualities at work, or to tease with a hint of something fascinating, some glimmering facet in the mostly opaque dimensions of an idea.

The transition between romantic and philosophic schooling was usually the most difficult to negotiate within the school. Partly this was because the age at which students began to use the language of theoretic abstractions varied quite a lot. Not that students were in tight age cohorts at this time, but even within groups that seemed entirely coherent in their interests and engagements earlier, it was unpredictable at what point the power of abstract ideas became potent for individual students. And partly it remained true, despite the best efforts of IE theoreticians and experimental researchers, that for a significant proportion of students the abstract realm never vividly came into focus the way it did for most. But it was the case that the techniques of IE teaching could ensure that all students at least got some distinct sense of a philosophic approach to the world.

Schooling during this time in students' lives tended to become a more serious enterprise. Not that it hadn't been seen as serious earlier as well, but it now became a matter of dealing also with the ideas that were publicly important and in which the students were themselves deliberately being encouraged to become agents. This prominently theoretic phase of education tended to begin for many students rather earlier than in previous decades, as effective IE techniques were developed for stimulating the appropriate tool kit. By the mid-2050s, a small number of students would move into this distinctive kind of intellectual engagement around age thirteen, with the majority following within the next two years or so. Fifteen or twenty percent of the cohort, mostly students for whom philosophic understanding never came to really dominate their thinking, showed only intermittent symptoms of philosophic engagement by age seventeen or eighteen. But even as theoretic engagements took hold, teachers ensured the continued stimulation and development of romantic cognitive tools.

This was the time for engagement with the theory of each subject area, and its most powerful generalizations. This was as true of the arts as it was of the sciences. It was also the time for intensive dialectical engagement — discussion and argument with instructors, with peers, with disciplinary experts and researchers and practitioners in all fields. University faculty, partly in response to the Salernoist movement decades earlier, recognized that it had been their own reluctance to have anything to do with schools, apart from criticizing their products, that had played some role in causing the "knowledge crisis" of the 2010s and 2020s. In the 2050s, committing time to working with schools was one of the activities on which university faculty received their performance reviews. And many faculty members admitted that they often enjoyed this part of their work most — the unstructured debates with energetic and informed young students kept them on their toes and contributed a dimension of expertise to the schools that helped exercise the students' philosophic tool kits.

All areas of the curriculum were explored in terms of the progressive drive toward apparent certainty that stimulated students' learning. As they learned increasingly sophisticated mathematics, science, history, literature, music, and painting, they had an undeniable sense of making progress. What else was that progress toward if not the truth? The power of theory was shown at work giving greater control over the content of all subjects. Students became increasingly more flexibile in their deployment of theories, capable of greater subtlety in challenging the theories that they themselves had formed; and the teachers who encouraged them were skilled in recognizing the way in which anomalies could draw the student to increasingly sophisticated theoretical thinking.

For most students it was a time of intellectual excitement. Earlier they had felt that they were seeing as through a glass darkly, but their theoretical concepts were cleaning away the impediments to their clear grasp on the truth about reality. In the educational process it proved a heady time, and also a somewhat dangerous one. Great pedagogical care was required to keep the students' intellectual development moving forward by gradually and carefully undermining the vast confidence in their theories and showing that the truths about reality that their theoretic thinking seemed to deliver were rather different from what they had supposed.

During the last years of schooling and during tertiary education, ironic understanding began to take hold, though perhaps only for half of any cohort. A lot depended on the interactions within students' individual social groups, families, and classrooms, and on their exposure to appropriate media, and relatedly and most importantly on the degree to which they had been successful in navigating the shoals of philosophic thinking. The schools and further educational institutions did little to deliberately stimulate ironic understanding, except in as far as they worked hard to help students recognize the weaknesses that came with the power of theoretic thinking.

That is a brief overview of the main stages of educational activities that formed a student's school career. It was a process that, in one dimension at least, became increasingly fragile as the student aged. Sensing the wonder of language and what it offered made the transition to mythic understanding compelling for all children; the appeal of romantic tools tended to allow an easy transition from mythic to romantic understanding; and the appeal of the philosophic tool kit was enough to draw most students to its distinctive sense-making — though that transition was harder than the earlier ones. But even more difficult, and impossible for some, was the transition to the ironic mode. The process of education, that is to say, became gradually harder as increasingly sophisticated tool kits challenged the student. While increasing recognition of the process of education in terms of mastering such tool kits made the pedagogical job clearer, it certainly didn't make the challenges go away. Education in those primitive centuries remained tough work for teachers and students alike. By the 2050s there was evident progress, but human beings had a long way still to go to learn how to adequately educate their young.

Entering a new school of the mid-2050s would likely have come as a surprise to an educator from as little as half a century earlier. One of the first surprises might have been the size and design of the schools. There were no schools of more than 150 students; classrooms were of varied sizes and clearly designed for different kinds of activities; many were arrayed on a single level around large central courtyards, in which there were a variety of gardening activities and structures being built and an area for the holographic representation of wild animals; very little electronic technology was in evidence in teaching spaces, though, of course, access to the I-net was immediately available if needed; a number of adults other than teachers would be evident; and instruction within classes would be somewhat unfamiliar, in the ways described above. New inner city schools were among the most interesting and varied structures architecturally. From the largely uniform and massive school buildings of no less than fifty years earlier, the exuberance and architectural wit of new school buildings was an outward sign of the profound inward change in the conception of education during that period.

Schools were places of talk, dominated by the conversation between generations and within generations. The human voice was the main agent of educational activity, and the natural world was the second. Technological enthusiasts from the beginning of the century would have been bewildered and disappointed to find that the machinery they had dreamed of delivering knowledge to students was given little attention in the schools of the 2050s. Talk, laughter, and emotional engagement were the core tools of the imaginative education that dominated schooling in 2060.

Conclusion

After all my research and reading and writing about the educational systems from the mid-nineteenth century to the mid-twenty-first century, my mind is overwhelmed with pity for how unbearably primitive the whole ancient process now seems. People at the time used to say that natural evolution was Darwinian but cultural evolution was Lamarckian — that is, in cultural evolution people could inherit the achievements of preceding generations. But so few did, and the massive enterprise of schooling from the mid-nineteenth to the early twenty-first century seems now just another of history's cruel jokes on our human forebears. All that boredom and pain, that half-learned and barely understood knowledge, which engaged the imaginations of the tiniest minority of people, the ill-directed energy of teachers, and the resentment of so many students. After more than a decade of their lives spent in these schools, most students could recall pitifully little of what they had been taught and had read; they knew by heart nothing more than the clichéd words of some pop song. The wonder of the world around them, the passion of their history, the possibilities of human experience were things of which they glimpsed only the most fleeting sense. After they left school most students never read anything but mental pablum again. Schooling during this time seems to have been a massive and clumsy industry poorly designed to carry the experience of life and the accumulation of technological skills across the generations. I am, of course, repeating many of the words prominent in the Vienna manifesto . . .

CONCLUSION

Oh well, back to the present reality, and away from that warm room on Sirius Five with its view of the colorful moons and the vast and fierce star in the distance. And back to our educational problems. That "future history," as I mentioned earlier, can be read simply as a fancy way of describing how IE is different from most current ideas and practices and how it can, even so, be implemented. That is, the future scenarios are also the present scenarios of teachers grappling with a somewhat new approach to the stubborn problems of education. The struggles to find the emotional meaning of topics we are to teach, and the use of various cognitive tools to engage students' imaginations, probing a topic till the right facts and ideas come to the fore, could have been described more prosaically as work currently being done by many teachers involved with IE today around the world.

Reading current educational literature, you will not find much engagement with the kinds of issues I have been writing about in this book. I don't take this as evidence that I am dealing with ideas off to the side of what really matters today: as will be evident from the chapters in part 1 of this book, the issues that exercise many educators today seem to me off to the side of what really matters educationally.

In the experience of those working with IE ideas and practices at the moment, it is clear that some teachers have real difficulties with simply being able to incorporate them into their classrooms. Some take to it as ducks to water, free to do what they have always wanted to do or have already been doing. Most teachers are able to incorporate some features quite easily, but find others — sometimes the most important parts — difficult. It's that emotional engagement with algebra (!), for example, that they find hardest. In recognition of this I referred to IE as a "boutique" style of educating.

Good teaching is not easy; it doesn't come on the cheap. It requires effort. That effort is reduced with appropriate training in IE procedures, of course, but it will never become automatic. The professional expertise of teachers, the above scenarios suggest, is tied up with their skill in knowing the subjects they teach and teaching them in a way that can engage the imaginations and emotions and humor of their students. IE is just a description of how this can be done within the constraints of the regular classroom today. This is another way in which the language of "cognitive tools" is not really ideal. Typically a tool is something easily taken up that gets the job done efficiently, with minimal personal involvement. The kind of tools to be deployed in IE do share that sense of making something otherwise difficult relatively easy, but the tools are tied into our emotions and deep understanding. Nothing casual there and, in the end, no fast and cheap route to implementation.

Given that the future is unlikely to show the good taste to conform to my narrative guide for it in the previous chapters, what can now be done about education? If you agree that the form of education described in this book is better than that which currently dominates our schools, and that it is also practicable, then the details I have provided of how we can go about teaching and changing teacher education, the curriculum, and the school provide one response to the question. Something can be done — why not help do it?

REFERENCES

Beard, Charles A. (1932). Introduction to J. B. Bury, *The idea of progress: An inquiry into its growth and origins.* London: Macmillan.

Deacon, Terrence W. (1997). *The symbolic species: The co-evolution of language and the brain.* New York: Norton.

Dewey, John. (1897). My pedagogic creed. *The School Journal,* vol. LIV, No.3, Jan. 16th, 77–80.

———. (1963). *Experience and education.* Kappa Delta Pi Lecture Series. New York: Collier Books. (First published in 1938.)

———. (1966). *Democracy and education.* New York: Macmillan. (First published in 1916.)

Diamond, Jared. (1997). *Guns, germs, and steel: The fates of human societies.* New York: Norton.

Donald, Merlin. (1991). *Origins of the Modern Mind.* Cambridge, MA: Harvard University Press.

Donald, Merlin. (2001). *A mind so rare.* New York: Norton.

Donaldson, Margaret. (1978). *Children's minds.* London: Croom Helm.

Egan, Kieran. (1988). *Primary understanding: Education in early childhood.* New York: Routledge.

———. (1997). *The educated mind: How cognitive tools shape our understanding.* Chicago: University of Chicago Press.

———. (2005). *An imaginative approach to teaching.* San Francisco: Jossey-Bass.

———. (2006). *Teaching literacy: Engaging the imaginations of new readers and writers.* Thousand Oaks, CA: Corwin Press.

Fodor, Jerry. (1983). *The modularity of mind.* Cambridge, MA: MIT Press.

———. (1985). Précis of "The modularity of mind." *The Behavioral and Brain Sciences* 8, 1–42.

Gardner, Howard. (1991). *The unschooled mind.* New York: Basic.

Gerofsky, Susan. (2004). *A man left Albuquerque heading east: Word problems as genre in mathematics education.* New York: Peter Lang.

Hall, G. Stanley. (1904). *Adolescence: Its psychology and its relations to physiology, anthropology, sociology, sex, crime, religion, and education.* 2 vols. New York: Appleton.

Harré, Rom. (1990). Foreword to John R. Morss, *The biologizing of childhood: Developmental psychology and the Darwinian myth.* Hove, UK: Erlbaum.

Havelock, Eric A. (1963). *Preface to Plato*. Cambridge, MA: Harvard University Press.

——. (1982). *The literate revolution in Greece and its cultural consequences*. Princeton, NJ: Princeton University Press.

——. (1986). *The muse learns to write*. New Haven: Yale University Press.

Hazlitt, William. (1826/1951). On the ignorance of the learned. In W. E. Williams (ed.), *A book of English essays*. Harmondsworth, Middlesex: Penguin.

Hirst, Paul. (1974). *Knowledge and the curriculum*. London: Routledge and Kegan Paul.

Johnson, Allen W., and Timothy Earle. (1987). *The evolution of human societies*. Stanford, CA: Stanford University Press.

Lamb, Christina. (2003). In Trever Mostyn's review of Lamb's *The sewing circles of Herat: My Afghan years, Times Literary Supplement*, May 30th.

Lamm, Zvi. (1976). *Conflicting theories of instruction: Conceptual dimensions*. Berkeley, CA: McCutchan.

Mithen, Steven. (1996). *The prehistory of the mind*. London: Thames and Hudson.

——. (2005). *The singing Neanderthals: The origins of music, language, mind, and body*. London: Weidenfeld and Nicolson.

Ong, Walter J. (1982). *Literacy and orality*. London: Methuen.

Piaget, Jean. (1961). *Comments on Vygotsky's critical remarks*. Cambridge, MA: MIT Press.

——. (1964). Development and learning. In *Piaget rediscovered*, Richard E. Ripple and Verne N. Rockcastle, eds. Ithaca, NY: School of Education, Cornell University.

Pinker, Steven. (1994). *The language instinct: How the mind creates language*. New York: Morrow.

Rorty, Richard. (1989). *Contingency, irony, and solidarity*. Cambridge: Cambridge University Press.

Rosenbluth, Vera. (1990). *Keeping family stories alive*. Vancouver, B.C.: Hartley and Marks.

Rousseau, Jean-Jacques. (1762/1979). *Émile; or, On education*. Allan Bloom, trans. New York: Basic.

Roy, Arundhati. (1999). *The cost of living*. New York: The Modern Library.

Russell, Bertrand. (1926). *On education*. London: Unwin.

Stewart, Ian, and Jack Cohen. (1997). *Figments of reality: The evolution of the curious mind*. Cambridge: Cambridge University Press.

Swift, Jonathan. (1801). On Mr. Collins's Discourse on Freethinking. In *The works of the Rev. Jonathan Swift, D.D.* Vol. 10. London: J. Johnson.

INDEX

abstractions/abstract thinking, 55, 70–72, 176–78

academic idea of education, 17–22; and concept of the mind, 35; and conflicting aims of other educational ideas, 9–11, 27–33, 35–39, 133–35; and curriculum, 18–19; and illiteracy, 19–20; literacy vs. knowledge, 20–22; Plato and, 25–26; as separate from socialization, 163–65; separation of academic and socializing activities, 172–73. See also traditionalism

agency, 74–75

anomalies, 75–76

apples (sample topic), 158–60

Arnold, Matthew, 18

Battle of Cultures, 113–15

Beard, Charles A., x–xi

beliefs, norms, and values, 12–17

Benda, Julien, 114

binary opposites. See opposites/ oppositional thinking

bodily tool kit. See somatic understanding

body-mind separation, 44–45

brain, 11, 38, 40–43. See also cognitive tools

calendar unit (sample), 98–100

Chronicle of Jocelin of Brakelond, The, 127–29

Chuang Tse, 126–27

cognitive tools: definition of, 40–43; education as process of maximizing, 40; epistemological, psychological, and emotional components of, 84–86; as five kinds of understanding, 43 (see also specific kinds of understanding); transition between kinds of, 178–79

Cohen, Jack, 16

colleges and universities, 106, 107, 131–32, 177

computer operating system (O.S.) analogy, 38–43

Condillac, Etienne Bannot de, 23

Core Knowledge, 89

Cost of Living, The (Roy), 10

culture: acculturation as aim of education, 9–10; Kulturkampf, 112–15; and language, 60; and literacy, 63; and the mind, 38–43, 84

curriculum: conflicting educational ideas and, 18–19, 32–33; impact of imaginative education on, 120–26; importance of exotic language mastery, 161–63; planning frameworks, 97–98, 102–3; progressivism and, 25, 161; relevancy of, 21, 92–93, 129–30, 133; separation of socializing and academic